Edward Everett Hale, Susan Hale

A Family Flight Through Mexico

Edward Everett Hale, Susan Hale

A Family Flight Through Mexico

ISBN/EAN: 9783744754590

Printed in Europe, USA, Canada, Australia, Japan

Cover: Foto ©Andreas Hilbeck / pixelio.de

More available books at **www.hansebooks.com**

A FAMILY FLIGHT

THROUGH MEXICO

BY
REV. E. E. HALE AND MISS SUSAN HALE

Authors of " A Family Flight through France, Germany, Norway and Switzerland," " A Family Flight over Egypt and Syria," " A Family Flight through Spain," and " A Family Flight around Home."

FULLY ILLUSTRATED

BOSTON
LOTHROP, LEE & SHEPARD CO.

CONTENTS.

	PAGE.
CHAPTER I.	
THE "CITY OF WASHINGTON."	13
CHAPTER II.	
HAVANA	20
CHAPTER III.	
LANDING	28
CHAPTER IV.	
VERA CRUZ	35
CHAPTER V.	
ORIZABA	44
CHAPTER VI.	
CORTES	51
CHAPTER VII.	
NEW ORLEANS	59
CHAPTER VIII.	
THE FRENCH MARKET	65
CHAPTER IX.	
LEAVING ORIZABA	69
CHAPTER X.	
THE CAFE ANGLAIS	75
CHAPTER XI.	
JUDAS	81
CHAPTER XII.	
RELEASED	90

1334038

CHAPTER XIII.
Toluca 95

CHAPTER XIV.
Anahuac 103

CHAPTER XV.
Morelia 109

CHAPTER XVI.
Mexican Churches 115

CHAPTER XVII.
The Camellina 123

CHAPTER XVIII.
The Aztecs 128

CHAPTER XIX.
Helena's Adventure 135

CHAPTER XX.
A Sudden Departure 141

CHAPTER XXI.
Lake Cuitzao 148

CHAPTER XXII.
Two Patriots 154

CHAPTER XXIII.
Mexico Again 159

CHAPTER XXIV.
Chapultepec 165

CHAPTER XXV.
Santa Anna 171

CHAPTER XXVI.
Death of Montezuma 179

CHAPTER XXVII.
"Noche Triste." 185

CHAPTER XXVIII.
MAYAN CITIES.. 195

CHAPTER XXIX.
NACHAN, — THE SEVEN SERPENTS................................... 203

CHAPTER XXX.
THE NATIONAL MUSEUM.. 214

CHAPTER XXXI.
THE END OF THE CONQUEST.. 224

CHAPTER XXXII.
LAST DAYS IN THE CAPITAL....................................... 229

CHAPTER XXXIII.
MIRAFLORES... 239

CHAPTER XXXIV.
DEPARTURE.. 247

CHAPTER XXXV.
MAXIMILIAN... 254

CHAPTER XXXVI.
OVER THE BORDER.. 263

CHAPTER XXXVII.
COLONEL INGHAM... 270

CHAPTER XXXVIII.
KANSAS... 277

CHAPTER XXXIX.
STILL MOVING... 284

CHAPTER XL.
CONCLUSION... 292

LIST OF ILLUSTRATIONS.

	PAGE.		PAGE.
Istaccihuatl from Amecameca	Front.	Plaza Santa Domingo, Mexico	118
Hazard Lighthouse, Florida	12	Cacti	122
Little Helena Johnstone	15	Ruins found in Yucatan	129
A Vision of Yucatan	16	Ancient Vase found in Missouri	130
Scene upon the St. John's	18	Montezuma	131
Tomb of Columbus at Havana	23	Ancient Aztec Vase	137
Banana	24	Querétaro	142
Flying-fish	25	The Morning March	143
Coral Reef	27	The Virgin of Guadalupe	144
Bird's Eye View of Vera Cruz	34	Ornamental	147
Vulture at Home	36	Birds on the Lake	152
Fernando Cortés	39	Castle of Chapultepec	164
Vegetation of the Tierra Caliente	41	Ornamental	170
Coffee Branch near Cordoba	46	Cypress Groves of Chapultepec	175
From the Tierra Caliente	47	Ornamental	178
View in the Island of Cuba	53	Ornamental	184
A Mexican Idol	56	Distant View of Mexico	186
Pyramid of Cholula	57	The Tree of the Noche Triste	187
Fruit	58	Fountain of the Aqueduct	189
The Jackson Statue	63	An Ancient Aztec Temple	193
Luxuriating	74	Governor's House, Uxmal	197
Ornamental	80	Bas-Relief at Chichen-Itza	198
The Viga	84	The Statue of Chac-Mool	199
The Cathedral at Merida	89	Palemke	202
Ruins	94	Tablet in the Temple of the Cross	205
Lake Cuitzao	99	Left Side of Tablet	208
The Sportsman	102	Right Side of Tablet	209
Quetzalcoatl	104	Statue at Copan	211
Ladies' Delight	113	Mayan Women	213
Ornamental	114	Court of the National Museum	215

List of Illustrations.

	PAGE		PAGE
Nezahualcoyotl . . .	221	Carlotta	261
Ornamental	223	The Execution of Maximilian .	262
Interior of the Cathedral of Mexico	231	General Manuel Gonzales . .	264
		General Porfirio Diaz . .	265
Ornamental . . .	236	A transient Passenger . .	268
Municipal Palace . .	237	Ornamental	269
Luxuriant Verdure . . .	240	In Monument Park, Colorado .	276
Ancient Temple . . .	241	A Kansas Railroad . . .	283
Interior of Car	248	Pachuca	287
Water-Carrier	253	Ornamental	291
Distant Tula	257	A Lake City	293
Benito Juarez	259	Quien Sabe ?	299
Maximilian	260	In mid-ocean	301

HAZARD LIGHTHOUSE, FLORIDA.

A FAMILY FLIGHT THROUGH MEXICO.

CHAPTER I.

THE "CITY OF WASHINGTON."

"YOU see this is really very comfortable," said Miss Lejeune, "and I am looking forward with rapture to having my stateroom all to myself. That top-berth, to which poor old Bessie has climbed so often, will now hold all my little things, and there is plenty of room under the berth and sofa for the rest."

"Well," said Clarence Hervey, with a sigh, "if you really like it, we can make no objection, but it seems rather forlorn to launch you off alone, even upon your favorite element."

These two old friends were sitting on the sofa of Camerote number five, steamship *City of Washington*, sailing from New York for Vera Cruz, via Havana. It was the nineteenth of March. The snow was falling in thick wet flakes; the deck of the steamer, and all the brass railings, ropes, ventilators, sky-lights, were covered with a white coating an inch and a half deep. Mr. Hervey looked out of the square window of the stateroom, and said:

"It is a dismal day too, aunt Dut, to send you off. I must say I think the skies frown upon your scheme as we have done."

"My dear Clarence, I love this weather; I would not have it otherwise. It heightens the effect of contrast intensely. Only think of the satisfaction I shall have in Mexico, when I tell them the snow was an inch and a half deep when I left New York. And now, Mr. Hervey," she added, rising, "I think you had better go, and I will hunt up Mrs. Johnstone and see if there is anything I can do for her. You know," she added, in a voice which broke a little, "I detest these partings, brief as have always been our separations."

They left the cabin, and ascended the curved stairway which led from the lower saloon, upon which the staterooms opened, to a place built up on the deck called "the Social Hall." As they passed the stewardess, a buxom, pleasant-looking English woman, Mr. Hervey said to her:

"You must take good care of this lady, stewardess; she is travelling by herself."

"Never fear, sir," she replied in a cheery voice, "we shall be good friends, no doubt."

The Social Hall was a dreary enough place, in spite of a piano, and a row of stuffed seats running around it beneath the windows. It was filled with a crowd of departing travellers and weeping friends, driven in from the deck by the discomfort of the bleak weather without.

"Good-by," — "Good-by!" A firm clasp of hands, and eyes that looked into each other full of confidence and affection, said more than words could have done of mutual encouragement and cheer.

"Do not let them worry about me at home," said Miss Lejeune at the last. "I shall enjoy everything; and Bessie and Tom will be in Mexico before me, so we shall soon have a merry meeting." She could not well follow her friend through the sticky snow to the gangway; from the open door she watched him as he crossed the plank, waving her handkerchief in farewell, and then as he disappeared, somewhat sadly she turned and descended again to the lower saloon.

Like the upper one, it was crowded with departing passengers and their friends. A babel of languages filled the air, thick with smoke from the cigarettes of the Spanish portion of the crowd. French Spanish, English, American sentences followed close upon each other and were mingled in general confusion. Miss Lejeune found little Helena Johnstone, who led her, with some difficulty, to the stateroom of her mother, Mrs. Johnstone, for the sake of whom, in a great measure, Miss Augusta had undertaken the present expedition, although her fondness for travel and several other reasons had made a "combination" which decided her upon it.

Mrs. Johnstone, an old school friend of Miss Lejeune, — and of Mrs. Horner as well, — had been married for about ten years, to an Englishman. During the greater part of this time they had lived in Canada. Not long before the beginning of the present "Flight" Mr. Johnstone received from the Queen an official appointment in Merida, which is the capital city of Yucatan. All the Johnstones came to New York for their outfit, and for a couple of months were in constant intercourse with

LITTLE HELENA JOHNSTONE.

the Horner circle, all of whom became interested, with their usual avidity for new information about lands and peoples, in the civilization, both ancient and modern, of Mexico, Yucatan, and the Republic of Central America. Mr. Johnstone was a well-bred, well-read man with a good deal of taste in archæological subjects. He entered with spirit and interest into his new mission, hoping to combine with it investigation and perhaps discovery in the interesting field of research in the antiquities of Yucatan.

Mrs. Johnstone was devoted to her husband and family, — not so much to science. This may be excused, from the absorbing care and interest demanded of her by two children of nine and seven years old, and a new baby, just a year old on the day of departure. She was a gentle little woman of great sweetness of disposition, without any superfluous force of character. For some years her health had not been of the best; it was hoped that

A VISION OF YUCATAN.

the milder climate and tropical attributes of Merida might render it more robust.

The interest which the Horners took in the Johnstone family helped much in making a New York winter tolerable to them. As for Mrs. Horner, she was perfectly happy. In possession of her own house, with all her family about her, she declared she should never stir again from her household goods. Late in the autumn, just in time to celebrate Christmas in their own country, the Herveys had returned to New York, and were pleasantly installed, keeping house, within easy distance of Mr. Horner's comfortable and hospitable ménage. The Hervey baby was the centre around which everything turned. Miss Lejeune even, who was celebrated for what may be called "an armed neutrality" in reference to babies, surrendered to the charms of this one and was known to have actually kissed it once, when no one but the nurse was present.

So Mrs. Horner fondly flattered herself that the wandering days were over. Mr. Horner appeared to have completely changed his character. What he now liked was to stop in and see the baby on his way down town in the morning, and to stop and see the baby on his way up at night. He could not bear the sight of a map, a guide-book or a time-table; foreign languages had become odious to him, and the only currency he cared for was good American dollars and cents.

But the Johnstones came, and the Johnstones' plans stirred the roving blood, and the thirst for travel still only dormant in some of the Horners. It was Bessie and Miss Lejeune who instigated the conspiracy. Miss Augusta was filled with compassion for her friend, the mother of three children, making a voyage with no other feminine companion than the nurse, or maid, who was to take the baby in charge. She boldly announced her intention of joining the expedition, with no thought for her own future after the end of the voyage; thereupon Bessie, with the aid of Tom, built a scheme for her protection and their own satisfaction, which will be further unfolded later on, for we must not leave Miss Lejeune any longer in the saloon of the *City of Washington*.

The ship was off, and gliding along smoothly through the snowstorm towards thick banks of dark clouds which hung all round the horizon. The steamer was well warmed with hot pipes, but the deck was intensely cold, and even under cover, as many rugs and wraps were needed as for the Atlantic voyage.

Miss Lejeune's sealskin coat and muff and heavy carriage rug were barely enough to keep her comfortable on the first evening when she curled herself up in a corner of the Social Hall, and tried to make out some of her companions, by the dim light of the lamps, swinging and rattling, for the weather was somewhat rough.

But in twenty-four hours all was changed, and on the third day

SCENE UPON THE ST. JOHN'S.

the passengers on board the *City of Washington* were sunning themselves on deck, and rejoicing in the softest of airs and loveliest of skies. Cape Hatteras, in the end of March, is held up as a dangerous and uncomfortable point to pass, but with the exception of some rolling and tossing for one night, there was nothing disagreeable. On Sunday they were floating tranquilly along the coast of Florida, a long, low shore about two miles off, which reminded Miss Lejeune of the Nile, — a line of white sand with bright green above it, broken by openings where rivers came down to the sea. Those of the passengers who knew the country described vividly the snakes and alligators with which it was peopled, for the part of Florida they were passing, is as yet almost inaccessible by any land routes, as railroads have not yet penetrated there.

The moon, which was new when they left, grew every night brighter. Awnings were stretched on the deck during the daytime, but these were taken away at night, and every evening was lovelier than the one before. No wraps were now needed, and thick clothing could be discarded. A pleasant little knot of people with whom it was easy to make acquaintance under such circumstances gathered upon the after deck, who, leaning back in their ship chairs chatted lightly of their various past travelling experiences, and anticipated the coming future ones. The captain, the purser and the first officer often joined their conversations. Wonderful were their tales about the sharks which abound in these waters. They are often caught from these steamers. The excitement of cutting open a shark fifteen feet long, is to see what is inside of him, for he swallows everything (like the listeners to this statement), and the captain assured Miss Lejeune that he had seen several whole chickens, a soldier's cap with brass buttons, two hoofs of a cow, and a tomato-can, taken out of one shark.

CHAPTER II.

HAVANA.

"IF you get up now, marm, you can see Morro Castle out of your window, right here," said the friendly stewardess; and there it was. Miss Lejeune kneeled upon the sofa of her stateroom, and saw the stately castle that guards the entrance of Havana, close at hand. It is very pretty, its solid outer battlements set firmly on the rock close at the water's edge. The lighthouse, more modern than the rest, forms a part of the buildings of the castle.

It was hard to stop looking from the window, but Miss Augusta made haste to dress. Arrived on deck, she found the other side was the more interesting, for there in the full glow of early morning light was the city of Havana. The fine harbor is like an inland pond, with a very narrow entrance. On the port side was Morro Castle; thence low hills, with some few palms, and the bright green foliage of other trees stretched round to the other side, where the low town encircles the bay.

It looked like Alexandria, in Egypt, Miss Lejeune thought; certainly very unlike New York. The houses were flat-roofed, and painted light yellow for the most part. The sunlight fell full upon them, and they stood out bright and clear against a sky of deep violet gray. The ship was already at anchor, a mile or so from the town, and swarms of boats were hastening towards it like birds of prey. They are called "canoes," but were large and solid, sometimes with two masts, generally with one far forward. Every one had a sort of hen-coop arrangement in the stern which could be covered with an awning. If it was up, however, the heads of passengers stood out between the bars, like chickens going to market. In a few minutes these boats were clustered about the ship, and dark creatures were swarming up her side, some of them "cargadores," employed to unload the steamer of freight destined for Havana, others runners from hotels; and the boatmen themselves boarded the deck to make bargains with wary or unwary tourists. Already trunks were being lowered into the boats, and a shout from a departing hen-coop drew the attention of Miss Lejeune to the pleasant Philadelphia party, going to stay awhile in Cuba. It was a misfortune to lose these agreeable fellow-passengers after a few days of easy intercourse. They were to be much missed the rest of the time, especially as the number of travellers was small.

Havana is the capital of the Island of Cuba, the largest and one of the finest, of the islands of the West Indies. It belongs to Spain, and is a colony very important to her. Cuba was discovered by Columbus during his first voyage. He caught the first glimpse of this "Pearl of the Antilles" on the twenty-eighth of October, 1492, and gave it the name of Juana, after Prince Juan, the son of Ferdinand and Isabella, who, unfortunately for the future of Spain, did not live to reign. After the death of Ferdinand, the island received the name of Fernandina, and again that of Santiago, in reverence for the patron saint of Spain; but the old Indian name has outlasted the others, and the island is known everywhere as Cuba. Havana, as Miss Lejeune said, is a word which shows how easy a language is Spanish. Turn it round and it means "a Haven." The island remained in the hands of the Spanish without interruption until the latter half of the eighteenth century. Havana was built early in the sixteenth century, its fine harbor, and the protection of the strongly built Morro Castle giving it a start over other towns, and in 1589 it became the capital of the island. In June, 1762, Havana was captured by the

English, but they occupied the place for only a few months, for by the treaty of Paris in 1763, Havana was restored to Spain. Yet in the brief time that the English were in the place, it is thought that they gave a start to its prosperity which it has enjoyed ever since. Its climate, and the great fertility of the soil, good for growing the sugar-cane and the coffee-plant, as well as tobacco, rice and cotton, would render Cuba the most productive of places, but at present the system of heavy taxes pursued by the Spanish government has gravely checked the prosperity of the island. There is an air of poverty and deterioration about the streets and Paseo, once so gay; the inhabitants are poor, depressed and discouraged, a certain melancholy pervades the air, belonging to a population without the spur of progress. Nevertheless, Havana is still a picturesque and most interesting town.

Miss Lejeune's Spanish, never very remarkable, was rusty with disuse, for it was two years since the Horners were in Spain. However, she managed to explain to a dark boatman who hovered about her on deck, very early in the morning, in a checked blue cotton shirt, tall straw hat, that "mas tarde," she might employ him. *Mas tarde*, therefore, — i. e. later on — when she had mustered her party, and the first officer had made for them a sharp bargain with him, they descended into his boat and were soon flying with spreading sail over the harbor towards the town, to the Muelle de la Caballeria. Crowds of small boats were fastened to the pier. Two broad steps led up to the landing. Passing by booths hung with bananas and oranges, they entered the walls of the town by an iron gate. Mr. Johnstone was with Miss Lejeune, and Theodore his son, commonly called Jack for short. Mrs. Johnstone stayed on the steamer with the nurse and the other children. Two or three other passengers came on shore in the same boat, and the little groups kept together to stroll through the town with that want of purpose which is sometimes more entertaining than a settled object in first entering a new place.

Near the entrance was a pretty plaza bordered with large green trees and tall flowering shrubs, delightful to the eyes of the New Englanders, who had seen nothing but bare branches and slippery sidewalks for the last four months. Here stands a small chapel and a monument to Christopher Columbus, both whitewashed, surrounded by an iron railing. Mr. Johnstone, with an impetuous devotion to the great discoverer, praiseworthy in an Englishman, was anxious to enter the chapel; but Miss Augusta's feeble Spanish wrested from a passing Cuban the information that the place is open for admission only one day in the year, the birthday of Christófero. The chapel is said to contain pictures representing events of the early Spanish discoveries. His tomb is in

TOMB OF COLUMBUS AT HAVANA.

the Cathedral, on the right side of the high altar. Columbus was first buried in Spain, at Valladolid; later his remains were removed to Seville, and in 1536 they were taken to St. Domingo. When in 1795 this place was given up to the French, the Spaniards resolved to retain the relics of their Great Discoverer, and the coffin was transported to Havana.

They went to a money-changers to get some Cuban money, to spend that day only, as it would be of no further use to them. Miss Lejeune was pleased to find she was to receive two dollars and forty cents, Cuban, for a one dollar bill of the United States; but as she immediately after had to pay fifty cents, Cuban, for five five-cent stamps to put on her letters, she decided it was about as broad as it was long.

They wandered into the Cathedral, the exterior not so hideous as it is sometimes described, but within gaudily painted in fresco with tasteless pink and blue decorations; the ordinary sights in the streets were what amused them the most, negroes, Cubans, whites, all dressed in the thinnest of summer garments, for the sun was very warm, although there was a cool breeze. They had the good luck to see a volante, a private one, new and fresh. It had two large red wheels with very long shafts on which the

BANANA.

hooded body of the carriage, made to hold two persons only, was hung, something in the fashion of a "buckboard" wagon. There were two horses, one of them saddled, and mounted by the postilion, a grand negro dressed in white with tall top-boots. Formerly volantes were the carriages in general use; the owners were so proud of them that they kept them in their *salons* or else dining-rooms; but now they have in great measure disappeared. The streets were lined with rows of open fiacres, like those in Paris, some of them shabby and tumbling to pieces, ready for hire.

At the Hotel Telégrafo, a delightful place of which the in-doors was all out-doors, opening on a patio containing tall banana plants, and bird cages, they came upon the Browns and the Heatons who had left the steamer early. They all met as joyfully as if they were lifelong friends who had been parted for weeks; thus it is with travelling acquaintances, a voyage especially brings with it a flavor of intimacy. The Heatons were surrounded by Cuban friends, the ladies in mantillas, with fans, whom they were about to visit in the country. After an excellent breakfast at the Telégrafo, our party took fiacres, and drove about the streets, with eyes wide open for picturesque bits; then they were taken to the shore where a strong surf was breaking. Across the narrow entrance of the harbor arose Morro Castle and its neighbor, the Cabaña, very pretty with its rosy coloring, Moorish in effect. At the Muelle, "Mas tarde," for so they had christened their faithful boatman, was waiting, and over a choppy sea, with many a tack, they returned, not unwillingly, to the good *City of Washington* which they had come to regard as a kind of home.

After this, everything was so changed that it was like a different voyage. The climate took on a tropical aspect. They sailed over shallow seas of light emerald green, on whose coral bottom they were assured great sharks were always hovering; flying-fish leaped about the ship. The deck, covered with an awning, was hot all day, and Miss Lejeune found her stateroom more comfortable than those on deck. "I spend my life," said the purser, "in trying to persuade people not to take staterooms on the sunny deck."

They were at Havana on Tuesday, and on the Thursday the

FLYING-FISH.

steamer anchored off Progreso, the port of Merida, the ultimate destination of the Johnstones. Here Mr. Johnstone left them, but it had been arranged that his family should go on to the city of Mexico, while he was finding a suitable establishment for them in Merida. It was now that the society of Miss Lejeune was to be of the greatest importance to her friend, who was thus to be left, for a time, by her husband and natural protector. Mrs. Johnstone saw him launched in the boat which was to carry him on shore with a sinking heart.

The Gulf of Mexico is so shallow around the coast of Yucatan that steamers are anchored several miles from the shore, only visible as a long low strip of sand and green. Miss Lejeune would have gladly taken the boat to Progreso with Mr. Johnstone, and as the steamer lay there more than twenty-four hours, there would have been time to go, by rail, to Merida; but she could not well leave Mrs. Johnstone at this time, and she contented herself all day with watching and sketching in her feeble manner the native Mayans filling their boats with the merchandise brought from the States. Load after load of bags of Indian corn and other merchandise were taken from the hold, and the steamer grew lighter and floated high upon the waves. She was glad on the whole she did not make the trip, for in the afternoon the sea was rough, and the boatload of passengers returned dripping wet, and very seasick with bobbing about over the waves.

The rest of the voyage was tranquil; there were two stops, off Campeche and Frontera; at each of these places the steamer was anchored ten or twelve miles from shore, and had to await patiently the intuitions of the folks on shore who sent out lighters to fetch the freight.

The telegraph from Progreso to Campeche, which announces the coming of steamers, was broken down; and there can be no telegraphic communication whatever between Campeche and Frontera, for the monkeys, who constitute the majority of the population in that part of the world, are determined not to allow interference with their civilization by telegraph poles and wires. They instantly destroy the lines as soon as they are stretched, by acrobatic feats, and swinging with prehensile tails, to such a degree that the enterprising telegraph companies have retired baffled from the field.

Miss Lejeune was charmed with this information given by the captain in his most genial manner. "How different," she exclaimed, "how superior to the supineness of the New Yorkers and Bostonians, who allow their roofs to be stretched with wires in every direction. Why! in Boston, there is such a network of them overhead, that it is like living in an aviary, or behind mosquito bars — another nuisance, by the way, of our civilization!"

Perhaps she regretted this condemnation of mosquito-bars the next night at Vera Cruz; but this is to anticipate.

CORAL REEF.

CHAPTER III.

LANDING.

IT was sad enough parting with Mr. Johnstone at Merida, and Miss Lejeune had hard work to keep the spirits of her party at a proper level for the rest of the voyage, in spite of the lovely weather and the beauty of the clear blue water over which they were sailing through the Gulf of Mexico. Mrs. Johnstone kept to her cabin for the greater part of the day, sometimes coming out to sit in the saloon between the staterooms, where, though dark, it was cool; and here the others often found her submitting to the comforting conversation of the stewardess, who was always ready to furnish the results of her observation and experience to those under her care.

Miss Lejeune and little Helena, and restless Jack on the other hand, passed most of their time on deck, where there was always enough going on to interest and amuse the children; as for instance, when one of the boats from Campeche brought out two ladies as passengers for Vera Cruz, each of whom had to be hoisted up on deck in an arm chair, with the American flag wrapped round her knees. One of the ladies brought a bright parrot in a tin cage, the other had a chafing-dish full of *cuculeos*, — strange-looking beetles which give out a bright light from their backs. A gentleman on board wore one of these creatures, alive, on his coat-lapel, held by a slight gold chain about its waist to which a pin was attached. The theory is that the beetles do not care to eat anything, ever, and are therefore happy and comfortable in chains, their lives one long between-meals.

As the ship approached Vera Cruz, the great subject of conversation and anxiety became the weather, for this is of the greatest importance on arriving there. A fierce wind called a Norther has a way of suddenly bursting in upon the loveliest air, stirring up the sea and making it impossible to land, for there is no good, natural harbor. Steamers are sometimes detained for days tossing up and down in full sight of the city without being able to send a boat ashore. Clear weather is to be hoped for also in order to see the white top of lofty Orizaba and its companion peak of Perote which should be visible for a long distance.

The *City of Washington* was fortunate enough to escape a Norther, although it came in at the end of a little bit of one which had been blowing about for a few days; the clouds left by it, however, hung over the shore, so that no wistful searching of the travellers could discover signs of the snowy peaks they so much longed to see. The shore was in sight when they rose in the morning, and as they slowly drew nearer and nearer, Miss Lejeune and the children kept their eyes fixed upon the outline of the pretty town, hoping for a glimpse of the mountains.

"If I knew how high up to look," said Helena, "I might perhaps pick it out of the clouds. Do you suppose it is up there, aunt Dut?" she asked, pointing to a region too near the zenith for probable mountain tops.

The stewardess, who was on deck, very anxious to have them see the peak, laughed at Helena, for although she was making the most of the wonderful mountain, she knew that at so great a distance it could not cover a great part of the sky.

The clouds were inexorable, and Orizaba was not to be seen. They had to content themselves with looking at the fortress San Juan de Ulloa which they passed upon the right, and soon the usual crowd of boats hovering about the ship occupied all their attention.

The fort San Juan de Ulloa, built by the Spaniards, was begun in 1569, and completed in 1633. Thus although begun in the time of the Emperor Charles the Fifth, it was not finished until after Philip the Fourth had begun to reign. This anecdote is told about it. Philip one day was busily searching the western horizon with a telescope, and some one asked him what he was doing.

"I am looking," he replied, "for my castillo in front of Vera Cruz. I have spent so much money on it that I think it should be visible by this time."

The coast is low and bare, but the town sparkles in the sunlight, being chiefly built of white houses, relieved by the spires and domes of many churches. The long red roofs of the railway buildings add a good effect of color. Even without the snow peaks behind it, it was a pretty sight.

"Be sure to have your baggage with you in the same boat," was the direction of a wise adviser to Miss Lejeune about landing at Vera Cruz. With the friendly aid of one of the officers of the ship, she picked out a dark boatman from the crowd gathered about the steamer. As soon as they were allowed to come on board, she attached herself to him, and led him about to their different staterooms, until he had gathered all the pieces belonging to her party. She saw them lowered to the boat, then summoning Mrs. Johnstone, the nurse and baby, Helena and Jack, she marshalled them down the ladder and entered the boat herself. It was large enough to hold them all, and all their trunks, and soon they were leaving the good steamer, waving handkerchiefs to all the friendly officers and servants.

"There is Larry! Good-by, Larry!" screamed Jack; and Larry, the head steward, a grim but faithful Scotchman, who had been very pleasant with the children all the voyage, allowed a severe sort of grin to illumine his features as he watched the departing boatload.

Other passengers were busy in other boats, each doing the best for his own interests. One by one they separated themselves from the entangling crowd, and put for the stone pier, not far off, of the town.

The hundred "murderers," convicts, shipped from Progreso, sent away from Merida "for their country's good," were pouring out of the hold from a square opening in the side of the ship. They looked like one conglomerate mass of rags and dirt, rather than separate human beings.

"It looks like molasses coming out slow!" said Helena.

At the custom-house there were papers to be issued, and slight formalities with keys and straps; these were soon ended, and then all the baggage was taken up by strong brown *cargadores*, and carried to the hotel. It was here that our party first made the acquaintance of Samuel.

Samuel was a tall, lank negro, very different in features and bearing from the Indian native to Mexico. He talked as good English as his race do in general, and served as interpreter to new comers. He fastened himself upon Miss Lejeune very early after her arrival, and as she was thankful for his assistance, he assumed at once a fatherly protection over her party which was on the whole an advantage, although it had drawbacks, of which the chief was that they were constantly paying Samuel for his services; for however often Miss Lejeune "settled up square," there was always another peso to be paid for something.

Travellers in a new land are an easy prey. They are not familiar enough with a currency new to them, to judge of the sums demanded of them, and they either pay absurd amounts for slight services, or wrangle over demands which are perfectly reasonable. Miss Lejeune alternated one of these methods with the other; and thus wasted both her time and her money.

But Samuel was very nice. He pervaded the hotel where they stopped. He appeared before them, even in the middle of their rooms, with timely suggestions. He was at the front door when they went out, and at the door of the money-changer's when they arrived there. He managed their baggage from first to last. As soon as they reached the hotel, Mrs. Johnstone shut herself up in her room, to weep, and if possible to rest. Miss Augusta was tempted to be impatient with her friend, who was entirely unstrung by the separation from her husband, and the fatigue of the voyage. There was, of course, much to excuse the poor woman, and Miss Lejeune, putting out of her mind the thought that she was useless as a companion for herself, summoned the children and carried them off for a bath, while the nurse and baby took care of each other. Samuel, as usual, was on hand to point the way, not far, to a bathing establishment, where they made the discovery that the baths in Mexico are admirable. Even in small towns, there is always a well-arranged, and often luxurious place of the kind. A row of little bath-rooms neatly furnished, fitted for water hot and cold, opens upon a gallery overlooking a pretty garden, carefully kept, full of roses, sweet peas, and all sorts of flowers, always fresh by reason of running water, and blossoming all the year round in the genial Mexican climate.

An Indian boy brings plenty of towels, a little pat of very good Mexican soap, and a round wisp of maguey of fibres which takes the place of a sponge. It is shaped like a bird's-nest, and is soft and pleasant to the skin.

It was two in the afternoon when the travellers left the ship; by the time they returned from the bath, refreshed and joyful, it was nearly time for dinner, — their first meal on terra firma.

Mrs. Johnstone took nothing but a little soup sent to her room; but Jack and Helena, as well as their protector and guide, were able to do full justice to the food, which might have been called "fairly good," or "pretty bad," according to the temperament and digestive powers of the critic. The children thought it "perfectly splendid." Miss Lejeune was too tired to be critical. Her head still rocked with the motion of the boat, and she was a little burdened with the responsibility of the whole party resting upon her shoulders

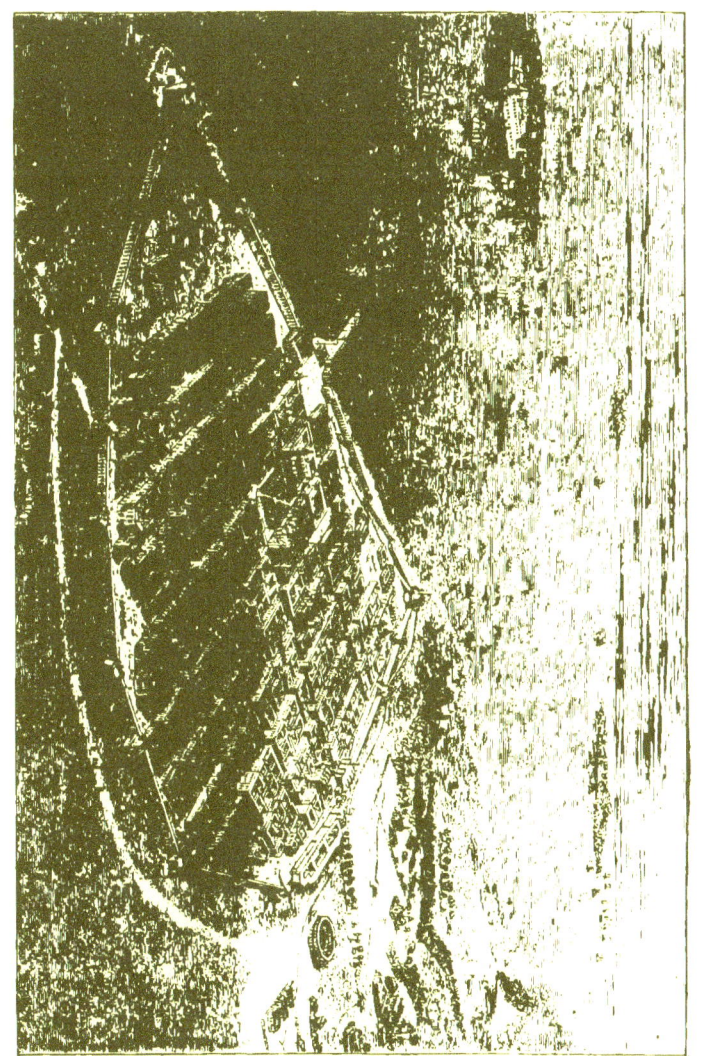

BIRD'S EYE VIEW OF VERA CRUZ.

CHAPTER IV.

VERA CRUZ.

ON arriving in a new country, the first city appears to a traveller more strange, more characteristic of the country than any other does afterwards, and thus the impression remaining in his mind of that city is not altogether just. As Alexandria had seemed to the Horners very oriental, so now Miss Lejeune found Vera Cruz most Mexican. If she should go back there after seeing other towns more remote from modern cosmopolitan influences, she would pronounce it, doubtless, as the Horners found Alexandria the second time, rather commonplace.

Like other Mexican cities, Vera Cruz is laid out in straight wide streets at right angles with each other; the houses are in general only two stories high, with large windows, opening each on its own little balcony; bright green blinds and colored awnings made the white painted rows of buildings gay,— almost glaring. The streets are very clean; and what keeps them so is the scavenger-band of vultures, called *Sopilotes*,— great blackbirds as big as turkeys that hover about the town and pervade the streets like pigeons in old Boston or pigs in Cincinnati. These birds are regarded by some travellers with disgust, but the Johnstone children thought them beautiful, and, indeed, the groups of these black creatures, perched upon roof or balcony, their black feathers and bold attitudes standing out against the light walls, were to Miss Lejeune picturesque and attractive. The hotel was upon a public square, or *zocolo*, and its large, very high rooms looked down upon banana-trees, eucalyptus and other tall growing plants through which gleamed beds of bright flowers. The cathedral with dome and tower, the latter hung with large green bells, rose on one side, on the other a row of white houses, with arcades on the sidewalks.

As it grew dark, the full moon rose behind the cathedral, whose huge dome stood out black against the bright sky behind. At eight o'clock the band in the zocolo began to play. Miss Lejeune sat in her high balcony listening to the music. The city-bands of Mexico are excellent, and even smaller towns than Vera Cruz have open-air music on one or two evenings of the week. The people all turned out on this occasion, and in the dim light of the street-lamps, the children saw them walking slowly round and round in close procession; ladies fanning themselves in light dresses and mantillas, gentlemen in white coats, officers in uniform, while outside the square the lower part of the population stood and looked on and

VULTURE AT HOME.

listened. Between the pieces the hum and babble of the crowd rose to the balcony. The air was soft and warm as summer, yet it was only the thirtieth of March. They recalled the snowstorm out of which they sailed from New York and shuddered and rejoiced at once.

Miss Lejeune ordered refreshing lemonade, made of limes, not lemons, and by and by the children went to bed, tired enough. She lingered till ten, when the music ceased, and then was glad to rest.

But there was no sleep, for mosquitoes pervaded the room, and continued the concert in the moonlight. The beds were hung with netting, but apparently the musicians preferred the inside of the nets, and found easy access. Miss Augusta, for one, was glad when four o'clock came. By the light of a feeble candle she dressed, and was ready to go to the door when long Samuel knocked, and demanded the small baggage. All their large trunks had been sent to the station the day before in a funny little cart with only two wheels, like a hand-cart, drawn by a spiked team of two mules and a pretty little fawn-colored jackass harnessed in front; a brown boy in white loose garments rode on one of the mules. As in most Mexican cities, there is a tramway, with street-cars drawn by mules, from the hotel to the station, and Mrs. Johnstone, with nurse and baby, was not afraid to go that way, for several Americans their steamer companions did also, while the rest preferred to walk the short distance, with Samuel always at their heels. They quietly left the hotel, where everybody was asleep, except one yawning waiter, and were soon at the station. Opposite, on the street-corner, was a café, in which, seated at round tables, was everybody with whom they had been travelling since they left New York. Native waiters hurried from one to another pouring out simultaneous coffee and hot milk from huge tin coffee pots. The tables were piled with good kinds of rolls and sweet cakes, fresh from the oven. The variety of bread, in different shapes, more or less shortened or sweetened, is very great in Mexico.

The hotels do not furnish early breakfasts, but at or near the station, coffee hot and good, is always to be found, a very good plan, for there is a sense of hurry at the hotel, whereas after the station is reached, you have all the time there is till the train starts. The baggage had been weighed and paid for the day before; Samuel now put all the small pieces into the car, and at last, having received for the third or fourth time the very last peso, he drew back and smiled upon them from the distance as the train rolled out of the station.

The Vera Cruz Road, or Mexican Railway, the first railroad made in the country, is an English road, built by English capital and engineers. The continuous line from Vera Cruz to the city of Mexico was opened in 1873. The ascent is so great to the capital that the enterprise was a difficult one, and the work in some places is wonderful, affording glimpses of grand scenery, as the train winds about the steep mountain sides.

At first the carriages on this road were like those in England, compartment coaches, but now they are replaced by long cars like those on railroads in the United States. And there were seated, adjusting their effects, as the train started in the early morning light, almost all the passengers of the *City of Washington;* for no one stays in Vera Cruz. The little French widow with the peaked bonnet, and her pretty, but sometimes soiled little son Ricardo, the Englishman, the German doctor, the lady who had joined her husband, the lady who had no husband to join, — these, and other minor characters, were in the same car with the Johnstones, and in another were all the theatrical troupe from Havana.

The first part of the way was uninteresting. The road led through long dreary plains of sand, dry and bare. It was inevitable to think and talk of Cortés and his expedition from Vera Cruz to Mexico, under circumstances much less favorable than those of our travellers, although they found cause for grumbling in heat and dust and fatigue; but their train was rattling them over the way at the rate of twenty or thirty miles an hour, in a car with crimson velvet seats and plate glass windows, a supply of fresh water constantly at hand, and refreshing fruits, bread and palque furnished for a trifle every few miles; while poor old Cortés and his men suffered many privations.

Cortés reached the island of San Juan de Ulloa on the twenty-first of April, 1519, and disembarked the next day on the Sandy Plain called by the natives Chalchiuhcuecan, but it was not until the sixteenth of August, 1519, that he was fairly started for the city of Mexico. The direction he took was not the same as that pursued by the railway, for he went towards Jalapa, a town not on the direct road, although a branch now leads to it. The description, however, of his first expedition from Vera Cruz agrees very well with what our travellers saw:

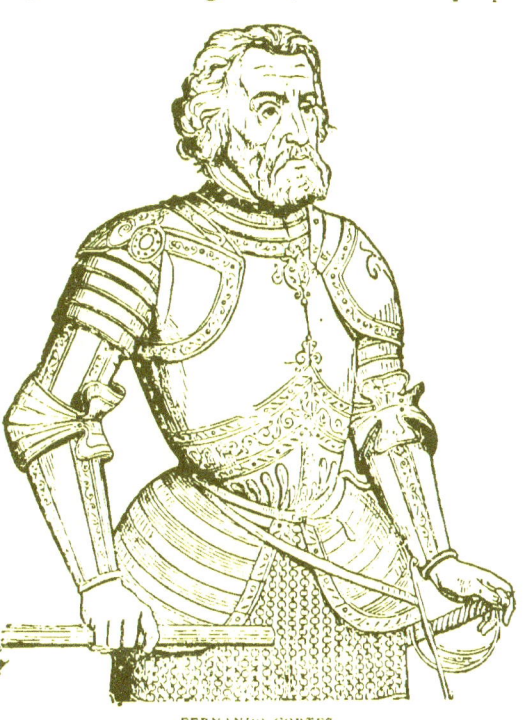

FERNANDO CORTES.

"The road lay for some miles across the dreary plains in the neighborhood of the modern Vera Cruz. In this sandy waste no signs of vegetation met their eyes, which, however, were occasionally refreshed by glimpses of the blue Atlantic, and by the distant view of the magnificent Orizaba, towering, with his spotless diadem of snow, far above his colossal brethren. As they advanced the country gradually assumed a greener and richer aspect. . . . They came in view of very different scenery,— wide, rolling plains covered with a rich carpet of verdure, and overshadowed by groves of cocoas and feathery palms."

Cortés had with him four hundred Spaniards, and only fifteen horses with seven pieces of artillery. Besides these, were thirteen hundred Indian warriors and a thousand *tamanes* or porters given him by the friendly cacique of Cempoalla, to drag the guns and transport the baggage. This strange band wound its way up the steep slopes, reaching Jalapa at the close of the second day. This town enjoys a fine and temperate climate, and the foreign merchants who live in Vera Cruz have summer places there, to escape the dangers of fever. It stands at an elevation where the breezes rising from the ocean keep the air and vegetation fresh all the year round. The Cofre de Perote, thirteen thousand four hundred and fourteen feet, and the volcano *Citlaltepetl*, "Star-mountain," which is the same as Orizaba, seventeen thousand three hundred and sixty-eight feet above the ocean, are both to be seen from Jalapa, and below, stretching down to the sea-line the splendid tropical growth of the *tierra caliente*, or warm lands.

As they ascended they experienced a most disagreeable change of climate, cold winds, and drenching rain, with a wild and dreary aspect, and had to work their way over the spur of the old volcano Perote, through lava and cinders, along the edges of precipices two or three thousand feet deep, for three days.

By this time they had ascended to a level of more than seven thousand feet, and were on the great table-land which stretches for hundreds of miles, with an agreeable climate and the vegetation of temperate zones. Here the Spaniards took the road to Tlascala, where they were detained for a long time. Our friends,

VEGETATION OF THE TIERRA CALIENTE.

interrupted by no hostile enemies, stopped for the simple reasons of fatigue and curiosity at the little town of Orizaba, on a level of four thousand feet above the sea, having made the distance in four hours.

After the train left the dry sandy neighborhood of Vera Cruz and began to ascend, the view from the windows was a constant succession of rich vines hanging in festoons upon the trees and bright with large flowers, most of which were new to the travellers. They longed to stop the train and gather them. Some of the trees seemed to have green leaves, but were solid masses of pink and white blossoms. Bright red leaves (probably poinsettia) gleamed from dark foliage, and whiffs of rich perfume reached the platform of the car as they flew by.

It is not safe, after the first of April, to linger in the *tierra caliente;* and so they had to leave all these tropical delights, passing through Cordoba where there is a wonderful view of the peak of Orizaba, and alighted at the next station, the town itself which gives this name to the mountain.

CHAPTER V.

ORIZABA.

MISS LEJEUNE'S plan, arranged before Mr. Johnstone left the party, in fact before they left New York, was to break the journey between Vera Cruz and Mexico by stopping at Orizaba. It is a good plan, recommended by all experienced travellers. The long dusty day in the train is fatiguing, for it is quite fourteen hours to the city of Mexico; and besides it is thought well to take the change of air gradually. The difference in altitude from Vera Cruz to the capital is great, for the city is seven thousand three hundred and forty-seven feet above sea-level. People often experience unpleasant sensations from the change, if it comes upon them suddenly; but by making a break for a few days, they become acclimated. Moreover as Miss Lejeune's excursion through the country was but a short one, this was the only chance of seeing the pretty town, which it would be a pity to lose.

Accordingly, about ten o'clock, after four hours in the train, quite enough, since it was hot and dusty, and the children were growing restless, they gathered together all their wraps, and left the car at the Orizaba station. Jack proved manful in lifting out his mother's heavy portmanteau. They waved hasty farewells to their travelling acquaintances, who were all going farther on, and then turned to walk along the platform to the small station, which is very much like those on other railroads, prettily accompanied with a little garden carefully kept. There was a crowd of people on the platform, for the down-train from the city of Mexico was just leaving also.

As Miss Lejeune looked about her for somebody to take the baggage, two familiar forms separated themselves from the group. She could hardly believe her eyes, but certainly that gentleman was Tom, and the lady with him must be, — Bessie!

The meeting was most unexpected. Her first emotion rather than surprise, was one of intense relief, for her undertaking had lately begun to weigh upon her, in a manner rather unusual to Miss Lejeune.

"You dear children! How did you come here! How did you know!" etc., etc., poured from her lips, as she kissed and embraced the pair, continuing with the same breath:

"Here are the children and the boys, and here comes Mrs. Johnstone. I suppose we can find some cargadores to take them."

"This is my man," replied Tom; "don't you worry, aunt Dut," and he beckoned to his brown follower, who at once shouldered everything, and showed a wonderful gift for hanging himself about with umbrellas, bags, rugs and portmanteaus.

Tom led the way, while Bessie was greeting Mrs. Johnstone through the station. There they found the tramway, and a row of cars harnessed with mules. Into one of these all the hand-baggage, heavy and light, were placed, and the party entering seated themselves. Trunks were to follow later. In a few minutes the car started off at a gentle jog for the town.

It often happens in Mexico that the station is placed a mile or more away from the centre of a town, which is reached by tram-cars. The dust, smoke, and noise of locomotives and the other evils attending upon steam-travel are thus kept at a distance, and as the street cars are well-managed they are popular, and in fact very convenient.

"Why, Tom!" cried Miss Lejeune, "you manage everything as if you were living here. May I ask again how you came to be here, and how long it is since you arrived?"

Bessie and Tom both laughed joyfully, and first one and then the other talking, they explained:

"When we found you were leaving on the nineteenth, which was earlier than we expected"— said Tom.

"Yes, I know," interrupted Miss Lejeune, "on account of the steamer I wanted not sailing the next week."

"We thought," continued Bessie, "that it would be horrid for you to be all alone in Mexico. I mean without any man."

"We were with her!" cried Jack, "and mamma!"

"Yes, I know," said Bessie; "but you know aunt Dut likes to have a great grown-up gentleman to mind what she says, and carry the umbrellas."

"So," said Tom, "as we had had about enough of New Orleans, and quite enough of the Exhibition, we started off at once, by steamer."

"So you, too, have been at Vera Cruz!" cried aunt Dut.

"To be sure."

"And saw Samuel?" asked Helena.

"Nobody else," said Tom. "This was a week ago, but we went straight on up to Mexico, hoping for news of you. They were expecting you at the Café Anglais, but thought you would stop over at Orizaba, so we came back down here, and have been here three days now," he continued, turning to Miss Lejeune.

"I telegraphed here yesterday," was her reply.

"Yes; and they have the despatch, and your rooms are all ready. I came down to the station on the chance, Saturday, but nobody has really ever heard of a steamer arriving so early."

"And if," said Bessie, "you had been fixed to go on to Mexico to-day, we should have been all ready to jump on the train with you, but as the telegram came we knew it was all right."

COFFEE BRANCH NEAR CORDOVA.

By this time, the car was trundling into the town. They found themselves in a long, straight, wide street of low houses in a broad, flat level around which on all sides arose mountains which elsewhere would be considered respectable in height, although they were not snow-capped.

"I hope you all looked your fill upon the peak," said Bessie, "for you know we do not see it from the town."

"Not see the mountain!" exclaimed Miss Lejeune; "I thought we were going to sit and sketch it all the time!"

It is disappointing that low foot-hills hide the snowy peak of Orizaba from the centre of the town of the same name.

FROM THE TIERRA CALIENTE.

There is a fine view of it from Cordoba, lower down; but the climate is unsafe in spring, as it is in the *tierra caliente;* besides the hotels there are not endurable; otherwise Cordoba would be a pleasant place to stay in.

The car stopped directly in front of the hotel. The landlord came out bowing, and soon the party were installed in comfortable rooms. The view from the windows was most charming. Even Mrs. Johnstone, who had all day been brighter and more like herself than at any time since parting from her husband, expressed pleasure at the sight, and sinking into her rocking-chair before her balcony, sighed and said, "This is really lovely; I think I shall enjoy it."

After Bessie had lingered by her side for a few cheering words, she left her, urging her to rest for a while, and then joined Miss Lejeune. These two, it may well be imagined, had much to talk about, and leaving portmanteaus untouched, almost without taking off their hats, they compared notes and described experiences, till Tom, who had carried the children off for a ramble in the town, knocked on the door to tell them *almuerzo* was ready.

"That sounds like Spain!" said Miss Lejeune.

"Yes," replied Bessie, "but Mexico is not the least like Spain; that is, Tom and I think so."

"It is more like Spain than it is like Vermont," suggested Miss Lejeune.

"That's so," replied Bessie with a Yankee drawl brought to her mind by this reference to Vermont. "Brush your hair, aunt Dut, and I will go and call Mrs. Johnstone. I mean to give my whole mind to cheering her up."

"Poor soul," said Miss Lejeune. "She was overtired, I suspect, before leaving home; and this is the first time she has been separated from her husband since their marriage."

There is a certain general similarity with individual differences, between the hotels of Mexico, as Miss Lejeune, now looking at her second, was beginning to observe. This one, like the rest of them, was built round a patio, or open court, where banana and other trees grew, a little fountain played, birds sang in cages, and geraniums with bright blossoms flourished. They passed from the street under a doorway to enter this patio, and crossing it, found opposite it the broad stairway which led up to the next story. Here a broad corridor ran around the four sides of the patio, lighted from above, and open to the sky. Upon the corridor opened all the rooms; those in front were the pleasantest, as they faced the street and looked across it to the beautiful view of bright green tobacco fields and sloping mountains. The rooms were high-studded; the doors huge double-doors, with rings for handles, keys as large as Blue-beard's, that did not lock, and great bolts besides that did not bolt. Directly opposite the door came the window, also a double window, opening casement-wise to the ground and leading to a little balcony just wide enough for two chairs; every room has its own balcony, unconnected with any other. Often, when tempted by music in the street, or moonlight, one of the party stepped forth upon his balcony, he found all the other balconies in the row occupied by the rest of the family drawn by the same attraction. The lower story is so high that the balconies are a good distance from the street. At Orizaba, this enabled the guests to overlook the very low buildings opposite, and enjoy the stretch of meadows, and the varied lights and shadows upon the mountain-sides. There are two little iron beds in every room; the floor is commonly of brick, with a strip of carpet before each bed. The furniture is plain, and somewhat meagre; but there is plenty of water, and the towels are excellent. There is always a rocking-chair, for this Yankee invention is dear to the hearts of the Mexicans.

Almuerzo was served in the corridor below, next to the patio. This space is quite wide enough to serve as dining-room, and it has the double attraction of being in the open air and under cover at once. The even climate makes this practicable.

As it happened, our travellers were the only foreigners in the hotel, and while they were in Orizaba, they scarcely met any one to talk to. Mysterious Mexicans occasionally occupied neighboring tables, but with these they had nothing to do. Novelty and fatigue were getting the better of all the new-comers; even the children, and Bessie herself was glad to rest.

"There is no hurry, as papa would say," she remarked, as they rose from lunch. "Let us do nothing to-day in the way of sight-seeing. I think I shall take a two hours' nap myself."

"All right," said Tom. "I believe I will write a letter; I may stroll out later."

As it happened, he fell upon his bed the moment he entered his room, and slept the sleep of the just until he was roused by the announcement of dinner. The nurse kept the children occupied in helping her to unpack such things as she thought they would need while they stayed in Orizaba, — thinner clothing than they had worn on the voyage, and their broad-brimmed straw hats.

CHAPTER VI.

CORTES.

IN the evening, they sat in the light of the moon, just past the full, which bathed their balconies, and flooded the valley and made shadows among the mountains opposite. Bessie assembled all the rocking-chairs in her room around the window and invited the family to come and chat there. Mrs. Johnstone had appeared at dinner in a pretty cap, a light knit shawl thrown over her shoulders, and joined in the conversation with some animation.

"Poor old Cortés had no good rocking-chair to rest his weary bones on his way to Mexico," said Bessie.

"Who was this Cortés," demanded Jack. "I want to know more about him and his fifteen horses."

"Only think," said Bessie, "the Indians had never seen any horses before, and so they were terrified when Cortés and his escort came riding along upon these great strange beasts."

"Do not they grow in Mexico?" asked Helena.

"What, horses? Not at all; that is, they never had before the Spaniards came; there are plenty here now, but their grandfathers and grandmothers were all imported, just as the Spaniards themselves were."

"Was Cortés a Spaniard?" asked Jack.

Tom laughed. "Bessie," he said, "here is an inquiring pupil all ready for your historic mania. Do you know," he added, "Jack reminds me of Hubert, with his English accent."

"Jack's voice and way of speaking are just like his father," said Mrs. Johnstone, with a sigh, "I think he is English all over."

"Who was Hubert?" demanded Jack, as much he had asked about Cortés. In fact he was an inquisitive child, always asking questions, and boring those who did not care to answer them.

"I should call Jack a regular Yankee, on the other hand," said Tom. "Hubert, my dear fellow," he continued, "was not one of the companions of Cortés, but a more modern hero, though of great prowess and wisdom."

"Stop, Tom," said Bessie, "you will confuse his mind. Let me tell them a little about the Conquest, and they will enjoy all the more the places and things we see later. You know about Columbus, don't you, Jack? and Helena, — or are you asleep, my dear?" As she added this she gently nudged the little girl who was sitting on the floor by her side, resting her head against Bessie's knee.

"No, I am not asleep, I am listening like everything," replied the little girl.

Bessie then began to give as full an account as the children could bear to listen to of the discovery of Mexico, and its conquest by the Spaniards.

"Columbus, you know," said Bessie, "thought he could sail round to India, west from Spain. He had no idea the world was so big as it is, and so when he touched land he thought of course it was India, and that is why he called the natives Indians, and why they are called so ever since. After his first discoveries, a great many Spaniards were filled with the idea of going further west, and by and by a man named Balboa reached the Isthmus of Panama, and saw the Pacific, another great ocean stretching far away. So the people knew there was a great country on the shores of the Gulf of Mexico, as we now call it, and they were always hoping to explore it, because they imagined they would find great quantities of gold and jewels there, just like the Arabian Nights. After Cuba, you know, where Havana is, that you stopped at, was settled, expeditions used to be started from there, and some of them brought back stories about the gold, and some specimens of it. So the Governor of Cuba, a Spaniard of course, sent to Spain to tell the king all about it, and to say that he meant to send an expedition to the new country, and take possession of it in the name of the King of Spain, who was, by the way, the great Emperor Charles the Fifth. The governor, named

VIEW IN THE ISLAND OF CUBA.

Velasquez, picked out Fernando Cortés to command the expedition, who was just the man for it; but afterwards, the governor was sorry he had chosen him, for Cortés, very naturally, wanted all the credit and the glory himself."

"And all the gold and jewels," remarked Tom.

"Well," replied Bessie, "he was pretty good about sending home ships full of gold plates and things to the King."

"Go on, go on," said Jack.

"Fernando Cortés was born in Spain, in 1485; he was a gay and lively boy, like other boys I have seen. He cared not much about books, and studied very little at college, and liked frolics and fighting much better. That was about the time that the Great Captain Gonsalvo de Cordova was winning battles for Spain, and Cortés thought of going to fight under him, but instead, it happened that when he was nineteen years old, in 1504, he sailed for the West Indies. There he stayed until 1519, always restless and wanting to be doing exciting things, and disappointed because he could not be picking up gold all the time. He was secretary to Velasquez, the Governor, and so it came about that he set out at the head of the great Expedition of Conquest. They coasted along the shores of Yucatan,—"

"As we did, you know, children," said Miss Lejeune; "don't you know I told you Frontera was near Tabasco, where Cortés was?"

"Yes; where the monkeys live!" cried Helena.

"Well," said Bessie, "there he had a great fight with the natives, and there he found an Indian girl, he named Marina, who was very useful to him forever after. But first I must tell you about the horses. Of course, they were all stiff and frightened when they first came out of the ships, but soon they were prancing round and very lively, and when they first appeared upon the scene of battle, sometime after it had begun, they produced a tremendous impression on the Indians. You see their riders had on helmets and armor that shone in the sun, and their swords flashed, and they came galloping along on these great steeds, all close together, fifteen of them, and the natives thought that man and horse belonged all together and were one terrible animal, all heads and arms and legs, as it were. The Indians threw down their arms and ran away as fast as their legs would carry them. This was an immense advantage Cortés had over the simple Indians. They believed the horses must be enchanted animals, and therefore immortal, and in his later fights with them Cortés kept up this idea as long as he could by concealing the fact whenever a horse was killed, by burying it at once. They were killed occasionally, so that the little supply of animals diminished, greatly to the regret of Cortés who could have better spared a few of their riders.

"Marina was a Mexican girl, who was sold by her unnatural mother to some traders, and they took her to Tabasco, where she grew up. So she could talk Mexican, which is different from Tabascan, and thus she was first employed as an interpreter, for Cortés had an interpreter, Aguilar, who could do Mexican, but not Tabascan, and he could translate Marina's Mexican into Spanish, for Cortés' Marina soon picked up enough Spanish to interpret by herself, and she became so useful to Cortés that he took her with him wherever he went. She was very pretty and attractive, and became perfectly devoted to the Spaniards; and her knowledge of Mexican manners and customs helped them out of many awkward situations. She was called Malinche by the Indians, and is still known in Mexico by that name.

"Through her, and the other interpreter, Cortés began to find out all about the country. He soon heard that there was a great kingdom called Mexico, high up on the table-lands above where he was, and that its monarch was named Montezuma. He resolved at once to go there and take possession of that kingdom, in the name of the King of Spain; a bold determination, with his little band of men, in a strange country, such a hard one to travel in, and the natives determined to resist him at every point. But he was the kind of man that loved enterprise and battles, and his men were fired by the accounts of gold and splendor at the Court of Montezuma. There was another thing, — Cortés was a very good Catholic, and you know the Spaniards believed in converting or getting rid of every one who had any other religion. It was then not so very long since Ferdinand and Isabella had conquered the

Moors in Spain, and the reason of this still made all Spaniards think that infidels were scarcely human beings, and must be either converted or killed. He was filled with a sincere, devout desire to establish the true faith, and set up the True Cross throughout Mexico. He found the natives had a horrid religion, which led them to make human sacrifices to ugly old idols, and Cortés resolved to do away with it, and establish his own. He called his faith the religion of Christ, but it was not exactly what we want you to consider Christian; for his was as blood-thirsty, almost, as that of the Mexicans. However, his zeal, in the cause of his religion, was sincere, and if he thought that tumbling over a few idols, and killing thousands of men, and leaving a cross on the spot of so much bloodshed, was the same as 'converting' a community to the Christian faith, he was not very much behind other people in power at that time, who might perhaps have known better, and did not.

A MEXICAN IDOL.

"So he marched bravely up towards the City of Mexico, inquiring as he went all about the country, and the people in it. They were not all the subjects of Montezuma, whose territory did not extend in this direction farther than the boundaries of Tlascalla which you can see on our railway-map.

"He had to stop and fight these people; but they hated Montezuma, because he was the strongest, and by and by Cortés made friends with the Tlascallans and persuaded them to help him. Then he went and conquered Cholula, killed the inhabitants and destroyed the temples, and raised the cross there; so that he was not ready to start for Mexico until the beginning of November (1519), although he landed at Vera Cruz the twenty-first of April.

PYRAMID OF CHOLULA.

"But now," said Bessie, "you children had better both go to bed. In fact, I think I shall myself. We must not let Cortés get ahead of us, and we have not been to Cholula yet."

"Do you think we shall go there?" asked Miss Lejeune. "I have been a little of the opinion it was one of those things it was just as well to omit."

"We have all seen the picture in the geography," said Tom, with a great yawn.

"The picture of what?" asked Jack, wide awake.

"The great pyramid," said Bessie, "which the Cholulans erected for their god Quetzalcoatl. You can learn to pronounce his name, and I will tell you more another time."

CHAPTER VII.

NEW ORLEANS.

"NOW really," said Miss Lejeune the next morning, "it is your turn, — I have been talking steadily all the time, and have heard not one word about New Orleans."

"Why, we wrote to you, didn't we?" asked Tom. "I don't remember whether I did, but I fancy that Bessie must have."

"O, yes," said Miss Lejeune. "I was favored with several communications from you, but each one began with the statement that it was much easier to tell about such things than to write about them, and then, after going on for a short way, each one of them ended up with the statement that you must now stop for you were going off on some sight-seeing excursion or other, and that you remained mine affectionately."

"I believe that must be about true," said Bessie reflectively ; "we did have lots of things to do, and it is much easier, as we said, to tell about such things than to write about them. It's hard, though, to know just where to begin. Do you want most to know about the Carnival, or the Exposition, or the French Quarter, or the Levee, — or what?"

"Don't begin about the Exposition," said Miss Lejeune, " for I saw the Vienna Exposition, and the Paris and the Philadelphia, and this must have been much in the same line."

"Only much finer," observed Tom, "oh! very much finer than any Exposition that ever was before, — at least, so a man told me, that I saw."

"It may be that it was meant to be finer when it was done," remarked Bessie, "but when we were there it wasn't really done at all, — some of it was hardly half-done, — and I don't believe it was finer then than any of the others, and I don't care much either," she added, being of that philistine class to which Expositions are trying and without interest. "Anyway, the French Quarter was finished when we got there and had been finished, I guess, for about a hundred years, — and never touched since, — it looks so queer. You go into it by Royal street, — Rue Royale in the old times, — and that runs straight through the whole quarter from Canal street to Esplanade street."

"Yes," interrupted Tom, "and they have electric lights in Royal street. Eight of them, a man told me. It seems real funny to go there at night."

"Oh! never mind them," went on Bessie; "you go up Royal street, which is quite narrow, and has balconies on each of the houses, and it seems very foreign indeed, — I don't seem to think of anything in particular abroad," said this young traveller reflectively, "but I never saw anything like it at home. All the houses have these balconies on them (except the great big ones and the very small ones), made of iron and generally painted green, and the houses are white or else red, so that the effect is so quaint and pretty, — you can't think. Sometimes the balcony is a sort of buff color; that's not so pretty as the green."

"The best of the balconies are on the Pontalba buildings in Jackson Square," continued Tom. "They are on the two sides of the square and the balconies stretch the whole length. The iron-work railing is beautiful; it is very fine and delicate; it has A. P. all over it, — Madame Pontalba's initials, — on all the railings of the balconies, and the transoms and everywhere."

"Jackson Square is right in the heart of the French Quarter," went on Bessie. "It's just off the Levee and half-way between Canal street and Esplanade, which are sort of boundaries to the real old French town. Then right straight away from Jackson Square and the river is Rampart street which makes the other boundary. I believe the old walls of the town used to run on Canal street and Rampart and Esplanade, and the other side was defended by the river. Those streets are great broad boulevards like Commonwealth Avenue in Boston, with a green in the middle. So you see the French Quarter makes a sort of rectangle with the river and these three streets, and Jackson Square is just in the middle of the side the river makes.

"And on Jackson Square opposite the river is the St. Louis Cathedral, which is really the centre of the Quarter, and the old Spanish government buildings made out of stone, and stucco-covered. They're really very quaint, curious buildings; they and the old Calabosa are about all that's left of the Spanish domination as buildings are concerned.

"In early times Jackson Square was really the centre of the city. The Cathedral and the Court House and the Prison and the Market,—oh! everything was right round it. They called it the Place d'armes there."

"It had a gallows in the middle," observed Tom.

"When did the Spaniards have possession of New Orleans, aunt Augusta," inquired Bessie; "they keep talking in books and things about the O'Reilly and the Spanish domination and the traces of it and so on, but I don't seem to know exactly when they were there."

"You ought to know better than I do," said Miss Lejeune. "I am rather hazy about the matter myself. I believe, however, that the French settled the city at the very beginning of the seventeen hundreds, and that the Spaniards obtained possession about 1760 or 1770. That was at a time when the French and Spanish thrones were in very close relations, both being held in the Bourbon family, and in some one of the many treaties and negotiations, Louisiana was secretly sold by France to Spain. There was some difficulty in the Spaniards obtaining possession, and your friend O'Reilly came in as a sort of conquering hero who was the first Spanish Governor to maintain himself against the people. Then the Spanish held New Orleans and all Louisiana too, which meant a full half of all we call 'the West.' They held it until 1800, when they ceded it back to France again. Napoleon, who was then at the head in France, felt that he could not keep it against England, and he sold it to the United States. That was a great feather in the cap of Thomas Jefferson, who was then President."

"Then the Americans began to come down the river, I suppose," said Bessie, "and changed it from a nice foreign town into a common American city."

"Tried to, you mean," said Tom. "It is not very American now,—the houses, some of them, are built, aunt Augusta, round a courtyard, just as if you were in Spain or here in Mexico; not quite so much as here, though," he added, looking about him. "And there are lots of these queer red tiled roofs."

"Yes," admitted Bessie, "there is a good deal that's foreign left in the buildings. There are the two old buildings on each side of the Cathedral, they are Spanish, and there's the old Slave Market in Congo Square, that's Spanish too. And some of the Creole houses in Frenchtown are built round a courtyard, as Tom says. You go into them from the street through a sort of covered passage-way with a lantern hanging from the top, and you find yourself in the open courtyard, with trees and shrubs and green things about, all surrounded on the sides by the rooms of the house itself, and on the front by the wall of the house next door. Then you turn to your right or your left as it may be, and there's the front door, instead of having it directly on the street. I think that's the way it is. We went into one or two that looked like that,— but the people don't live out in the courtyard much nowadays, I fancy."

"It was rather cold when we were there," said Tom.

"But tell me some more about the French Quarter," said Miss Lejeune; "you're very rambling in your remarks."

"Well," said Bessie, "to be exact, we may call the very heart of the French Quarter Jackson Square, which I won't describe, for you've seen the statue of Jackson, that's in that square in Washington, just across the street from the White House."

"That's Lafayette square," said Tom.

"I think the statue is just like the one in New Orleans. But that don't matter. On one side the Square is the French Cathedral. That's not very old. How old is it, Tom?"

"I don't know; 'twas re- built, I believe, about forty years ago," replied Tom, indifferently.

THE JACKSON STATUE AT NEW ORLEANS.

"It's rather picturesque, anyway, and has a garden behind it,— and the two Government buildings, one on each side of it. They are quaint, old, two-story buildings, stucco-covered; the three buildings make up together one side of the Square. Then on the two sides adjoining this are the Pontalba buildings. They all,"—

"Why Pontalba?" asked Miss Lejeune.

"Well, Madame de Pontalba was the daughter of an old Spanish Don,— the one who built the Saint Louis Cathedral,— and she was very, very rich indeed, and lived in Paris, and built these buildings. They're full of shops, and made of red brick, with green balconies all along the front; and all over the ironwork on the balconies, as Tom says, you see her monogram A. P.,— Antonia de Pontalba,— she only died about ten years ago.

"Then on the fourth side of Jackson Square is, — I don't remember just what's there, — I think there are some low buildings between the Square and the Levee."

"Isn't it funny, aunt Augusta," said Tom, "they say that the river is gradually leaving the city of New Orleans and moving away."

"Where is it moving to?" asked Bessie.

"It's changing its course. It goes away about fifteen feet each year. Don't you know the custom house, Bessie? That used to be at the water's edge, and now it's about two or three blocks in shore."

"That's curious," said Miss Lejeune. "I knew it changed its course sometimes farther up, but I didn't know that it did near the city. I should think they'd be afraid that it would suddenly make up its mind to move toward the city rather than away from it."

"I don't know what they would do then."

"Oh," said Bessie, "we haven't told you at all about the French market, — that's right near Jackson Square."

"Well, you shall tell me that in about an hour, if you've nothing else to do then. I've got to go up stairs now to see to my trunks."

"Do you mean to go to the bull fight, aunt Augusta?" asked Tom.

CHAPTER VIII.

THE FRENCH MARKET.

I'M given to understand," said Miss Lejeune, later in the day, "that the proper thing to do is to breakfast at the French Market on Sunday morning."

"Yes," said Tom, "it is. But we didn't get down there any Sunday morning. I don't believe Bessie breakfasted there at all."

"Yes, I did, once, if you call it breakfasting," said Bessie.

"You see," continued Tom, "they didn't breakfast at the house generally till about ten, and I used to get up early, or I did several times, and go to the Market and have an early breakfast there.

"The Market is a long rambling building, just beyond Jackson Square, with three tall domes on it. It's really three separate buildings, but you go right from one into the next, and the space between is full of people sitting round selling things, and of stands full of things to be sold and of heaps of all kinds of wares, so that it all seems one great place. They seem to sell almost everything; there is a vegetable market, and a fish market and a meat market; but they're rather mixed up together, and all in amongst are places where they sell cloth and nicknacks and pictures and boots and clothes and, — oh! everything; and all around are stands where you get coffee and so forth, and you breakfast at those stands. You get up on a stool in front of a counter covered with oil-cloth and tell the man what you want and he cooks it for you in a little stove, on the floor or up on the counter, with charcoal in it.

"You can have quite an elaborate breakfast there only you have to wander around to different places. I used generally to get some fruit to begin with and to eat that while I was wandering around thinking what I'd have next."

"I should think a foreign traveller like you might have been contented with your coffee and roll," said Miss Lejeune, "without wanting anything more elaborate."

"Well," said Tom, "when there was so much more for breakfast, it seemed a sort of pity not to have it. My favorite place was a stand with a sign that said 'The Morning Call.' I used to get coffee there and a sort of pie-crust kind of biscuit the man had. Then at other places I used to get other things. You could get beefsteaks or chops or thin broiled ham or chicken or fish,— there were lots of kinds of fish,— lots."

"They didn't have anything especially curious in the way of cookery. Not when I was there at least," said Bessie.

"They have curious kinds of bundles of vegetables," said Tom, "all sorts of things made up in a bouquet as if they had been the most expensive flowers. They had pieces of carrots and onions and lettuce and turnips and beets and other things I didn't know the names of.

"But on Sunday morning the people from the country round come in with all kinds of queer things. We didn't get there any Sunday morning; we always meant to, but somehow we kept not going."

"You haven't said anything at all about the Carnival," said Miss Lejeune; "you were there about Mardi-gras, what did you think of it?"

"Oh! of course we saw it, and it was great fun and interesting too, in a way," answered Bessie, "only not exactly as I imagined a Carnival. I thought all the people entered into the spirit of the thing and went round in masks and had a fine time; but they don't seem to do that. Carnival is more like a show or a pageant that the richer people give while the others only look on."

"There were some masks in the streets," said Tom, "but they were mostly black folks or children."

"Carnival seems to consist entirely of great processions in the day and evening and great masked balls afterward. All the people take it in, though, as a great holiday, and the streets are full all the time on Mardi-gras and on Monday."

"They have a King of the Carnival," said Tom, "Rex, he is called, and for two days he runs the whole city and does just as he pleases. The keys of the city are given to him, and I believe he really does the governing of the city for the time he is Rex, and he arranges the processions and things. Then the Knights of Momus and the Krewe of Comus and the Krewe of Proteus have processions too,— Comus didn't this year,— they have great torch-light processions in the evening and balls afterward.

"The king enters the city with great pomp on Monday morning. He comes from Arabia, I believe, and for some days before he reaches the town the papers have things showing his gradual progress, while on Monday itself they are full of orders and arrangements respecting his entry and his rule. He has a great retinue made up of dukes. Dukes of all sorts of places, as there was the Duke of Oil Works, the Duke of Upidee, the Duke of Pickings, the Duke of Creedmore, the Duke of Street-cars, the Duke of Dentistry, oh! lots of 'em. I don't remember all their names. They all enter the city on Monday morning, and at the City Hall Rex is presented by the Mayor with the keys of the city. Then this year they all went up to the Exposition on the river, where they had a great reception in which the king received the keys of the Exposition. Then for the rest of Monday and for all Tuesday Rex is the ruler of the city and nobody thinks of doing anything but amuse themselves. The streets are all full and a great part of the time the whole population goes out on the balconies to see the processions. They have one each evening and another one Tuesday morning. You know the processions consist of *tableaux* carried around the city on great *Floats*, as they call them,— great platforms modelled into different shapes to suit the tableau upon it. In the evening they are all lighted up by torches carried by negro torch-men in red clothes. The procession in the morning is given by Rex. The evening processions are given by the secret societies. The evening ones are the prettiest. We sat up in the windows of one of the Clubs to see them go up Carondelet street into Canal street. It was a mighty pretty sight. The Proteus procession, for instance, was made up of scenes from Chinese mythology. The floats were all sorts of fantastic shapes. The first was Proteus riding on a peacock on a mountain of silver and gold, then there was one float like an immense egg, one was a pagoda, and one was a tea-house. Then there were two; one of Paradise, and the next was the other place, with Chinese devils in it. They were very brilliant and splendid. All the figures wore queer Chinese masks and dressed in handsome and expensive stuffs, and the whole thing was lighted up by torches and colored lights so that it was beautiful."

"The Rex Procession," said Tom, "was all scenes from Ivanhoe. You ought to have seen that, aunt Augusta."

"Aunt Augusta ought to have gone to the Carnival balls and have had one of the maskers take her out in the quadrille. I wonder what he'd have said to her. We'll tell you all about the Carnival balls some time," said Bessie.

"The horse cars in New Orleans," said Tom, as a sort of wind up to the narrative, "are pulled sometimes by mules and sometimes by a dummy engine, never by horses."

CHAPTER IX.

LEAVING ORIZABA.

THE time passed very pleasantly at Orizaba, all the party agreeing that rest and quiet were a good preparation for future travelling. Miss Lejeune's leading thought was to fill up the time for Mrs. Johnstone, as best could be planned, until her husband should come for her. The climate of Orizaba is lovely; its average temperature for the year is seventy-two degrees Fahrenheit, and even at that time, — April, — resembled the best June days in New England, without, however, any fear of frosts, chill east winds or three-day storms. Day after day the same lovely blue sky, with fleecy white clouds, the same soft breeze, and bright, warm sunshine.

"Weather that makes you feel like doing anything!" said Bessie, praising it joyously one evening; yet as it happened they did nothing, or next to nothing, and left undone when they went away the chief wonders of the neighborhood. There is, luckily, perhaps, as yet no Murray or Baedeker for Mexico. The tourist is not nagged by the little book with red covers detailing the sights he ought to see, and the points he must visit. He has the satisfaction of finding out for himself his own lions, and every one knows that a very little lion which we have discovered ourselves, seems a more important animal than a much bigger one that every one else has recommended to us.

Orizaba is a city of about twelve thousand inhabitants. It is the capital of the State of Vera Cruz; for Mexico, like the United States, is divided up into States, each of which has its own governor and government. It is a flourishing town, with flour mills, a paper factory, all upon the three streams near it, but these business matters do not destroy the picturesque elements of the neighborhood. There are three pretty waterfalls to be visited. The valley seems like a large luxurious garden with the town in the middle of it, the flat-roofed, white houses interspersed with trees, and here and there the dome and tower of a church. The churches of Mexico are built universally with a tower or belfry, and a dome surmounted by a cross. The domes are sometimes made of colored glazed tiles, which gleam in the sun; sometimes they are gilded; otherwise they are a rich brown, harmonious with the landscape.

The first expedition of our party, in fact the only one they made together, was a very simple one, adapted to the capacity of their most indolent member, in this case Miss Lejeune, who was at this time singularly averse to expeditions, and loved her rocking-chair and her view so well that she never cared to leave her room in the hotel. But as the only exertion required was to go below, and step into a street-car directly opposite the front door, she yielded to the powerful arguments presented to her at lunch, and consented to go after a moderate nap.

The car can be seen approaching from all the balconies. It passed once in half an hour, and the children were watching, yet they missed the four o'clock car, and this was Miss Lejeune's fault, for her watch was wrong, her boots were not buttoned. But they caught the next car, and nobody minded waiting for it, for the sights in the street were yet all so new to them that they were sufficiently amused by watching the passing. Dear donkeys laden with sugar-cane, fodder, or chairs and tables, in short, any imaginable thing, women carrying heavy burdens on their backs, their heads covered with picturesque *rebozos*, a gang of laborers, convicts, working on the road, overlooked by a soldier in Mexican uniform. The street-sights through Mexico are all-absorbing. It is almost the only country left now, where the costumes are interesting. The native Indians are picturesque, brown, with gleaming white teeth and black hair, which the women wear in two long braids down the back. They are by no means a lazy people, lying about in sunny door-ways, like the Arabs in Egypt, of whom otherwise they remind you, but are always actively engaged, moving along at a brisk pace busy about something, and very often carrying a heavy burden, — like a bureau, for instance, on their backs.

The car came at last, and they seated themselves, bowing to the other passengers, who bowed and said, "*Buenas tardes.*" There was a lady returning from church, apparently, with her prayer-book, dressed in black, a mantilla on her head, her dark hair crêpé, and her cheeks slightly touched with rouge, and her face liberally powdered, while by her brown, ungloved hands it was evident that she was of Indian blood. A true Indian girl who came in, by and by, when the car was a mile or so out of town, was much prettier and more attractive. She had on a broad-brimmed straw hat, and over that her blue *rebozo*, — a sort of mantilla that covered her shoulders, but not too much to show her bare brown arms and neck. The rest of her costume was a white (originally white) chemise, and a white petticoat tied round her waist, and coming down to her feet, which were small and bare and brown. When she came in she smiled, showing her beautiful white teeth, bowed all round and said, "*Buenas tardes*," and then sat down on the floor of the car. The conductor pointed out to her that the other passengers were on the seats, and then she rose and placed herself there like the rest of the company. The car-track, laid along one side of the broad level country-road, seemed no encumbrance to it as it does in a crowded city street. Indeed there was plenty of room for all the things that wanted to pass, such as a drove of donkeys, a woman carrying a bunch of live hens home from market, and a group of horsemen. There are few private carriages in the smaller Mexican towns. The inhabitants like to ride in the tram-cars, and it is said that the *peones*, as the lowest class is called, prefer to go without a dinner, if they can, instead, pay the five cents that simple meal would cost, for a ride in a car.

The single mule (or more if needed) jogs along the way without much noise. There is no jangling of bells, and for some reason less heavy rumbling than with Northern street-cars. The conductors are not requested to punch with care, but sell little paper tickets which they take away afterwards. The conductors mix freely with the passengers and engage in friendly chat with them, and seem to be free from the mortal antagonisms by which they are supposed to be inspired in large cities. They are perfectly willing to have people enter and leave when they please. They carry horns which they blow on at intervals, and the tooting of these horns is rather wearing, but on the whole preferable to the endless clinging and clanging of bells, in the streets of Boston and New York. The road was bordered with huge trees, tall weeds and plants of semi-tropical growth, some of them bearing strange flowers. The hills on either side of the valley reminded the Horners of Interlaken as you go toward Brienz. The object of the trip was a pretty spot, devoted to a bathing establishment; there were a garden, and running waters, and fine old trees. The children ran about and gathered all sorts of wild things, — yellow, purple, white, growing everywhere, — and the elders saw constantly things good to sketch, for everything was sketchable. They had to tear themselves away for their return car, for the sun was setting, and it was dinner time.

On the return, the car stopped to take up two young ladies who were waiting in the road. They were unmistakable Yankees, armed with sketching stools, umbrellas, paint-boxes, their heads tied up in blue veils, and their hands neatly gloved. You might have thought yourself in East Gloucester, so closely they resembled the band of amateur artists that have lately clustered for the summer at that spot. Bessie eyed them with interest, but as she was at the other end of the car, exchanged no words with them. They left the car at the other hotel, on the side of the street opposite to the one our party had chosen. Before she left Orizaba, Bessie met the girls often, and scraped acquaintance with them.

"They are doing such an intelligent thing," she said as she was telling the rest about it afterwards. "They are not sisters or anything, only just friends; one of them has overstudied, and needed rest; they are both of them fond of art, in fact, they became acquainted at the Normal Art School in Boston, and so they had the sense to come down here last autumn, and settle. They have not stirred from Orizaba all winter, and do not want to. They have not been near the city of Mexico, and do not mean to until they are ready to go home. They did not know any Spanish, but they brought a Meisterschaft with them, and now they are fluent at it. Did you not hear them talking to the conductor? Their landlady, over there, is a German, and they both speak that. They are perfectly happy, and I approve of them."

"So do I," said Miss Lejeune. "How different from the wandering tribe of unprotected women that make travelling hideous by fastening themselves upon parties."

"Exactly," agreed Bessie, "and how much better fun they have, spending their little money, for I dare say they have not much, settled down here, and taking in the whole spirit of the climate and people, and all, instead of lashing about with a Raymond party, and being most dead, and all over with it in a couple of months."

"They may be millionnaires," said Tom, "for all you know about it, Bessie, and in that case I will marry one of them."

"They may," she assented, "but I do not believe it; anyhow they need not, in fact, they cannot spend much money here; the hotel charges are very moderate, and there is nothing to buy. Then they can wear the same clothes all the year round."

"I should think they might be bored, some of the time," said Miss Lejeune, "a rainy day for instance."

"Why, you see," cried Bessie, "it never is a rainy day, that is just the point of it. I fancy they do not care very much about reading, but you know they could have cart-loads of books here."

"And then the sketching," continued Miss Lejeune, "the landscape, and all the people, such good subjects, — and flowers, such endless flowers to paint all the time."

"Did you see any of their sketches, Bessie?" asked Mrs. Johnstone, in her soft, gentle voice.

"Well, the sketches, to tell the truth, were horrid," said Bessie, and she left the room to take off her hat.

CHAPTER X.

THE CAFE ANGLAIS.

IT was wonderful, the effect Orizaba had upon all our party. Mrs. Johnstone grew cheerful and wrote long letters to her husband not more than half-filled with longings for his arrival. Miss Lejeune became more talkative than ever, Tom more lazy and more amiable; he interested himself greatly in the Johnstone children and took Jack under his especial charge, teasing him a good deal, with a view, as he said, to improving his mind.

After several days of cloudless skies and perfect weather, they started off for the City of Mexico, taking up at the station the train that left Vera Cruz at the same hour they did the week before.

"*Hasta luego!*" they said to the landlord as they left the hotel. This answers in Spanish to "*Auf Wiedersehen*" in German, and means that you will come back again by and by.

"We really must come back!" said Bessie.

They started in good spirits, anticipating much pleasure in the day, and for a long time enjoyed climbing slowly with the train, winding round curves where the engine could be seen from the last car, and where deep precipices yawned below them, watching the vegetation change from tropical to temperate growths, until the country became bleak and bare. They had dinner at Esperanza, a station near the summit, and after that by a slight descent were on the great table-land of Mexico at the summit of the Cordillera which stretches for miles and miles at an elevation of more than six thousand feet, gradually declining toward the north. It is large enough to be a world by itself, and one forgets in travelling over it long distances by rail, that it is not on a level with all the rest of the earth. It has its valleys and lakes, and its volcanic chain, whose elevation from the table-land makes them conspicuous mountains, and whose height reckoned from the level of the sea places them among the great peaks of the world.

"Now for Popocatepetl and Istaccihuatl!" cried Bessie; "I hope we shall have as fine a view of them as we did the other day." But, alas! clouds of dust arose on the wings of a perfect whirlwind, hiding the landscape from their eyes, and filling them with pricking sand. A white film surrounded the train, sifted through the close-shut windows, fell upon clothes, books and everything.

If it were not for the name of the thing, they might have been crossing the Desert of Sahara; and this lasted for hours.

At Apizaco, a branch road leads off to Puebla and Cholula, but our friends were going on straight to Mexico. Two gentlemen came into the train who had done these places since they left the steamer; and Miss Lejeune greeted them with a cordiality which amazed Tom and Bessie who did not expect acquaintances there.

"I do believe, aunt Dut," said Bessie later, "that if you should go to the North Pole, you would be shaking hands with a grizzly, and telling him you knew him from his likeness to his grandmother. Now who are these people?"

"My dear, they are very agreable, and one of them is a great friend of mine. I dare say we shall keep meeting them." And so they did.

The two great volcanoes were absolutely invisible, but there were times when Malinche rose clearly from the plain, its somewhat symmetrical form covered with snow. It is a respectable mountain in height, fourteen thousand seven hundred and four feet above sea-level. They passed through Tlaxcala, where Cortés stopped on his way to Mexico, making friends with the chiefs and inhabitants, without whose help he could hardly have advanced upon the City of Mexico. It is now the smallest of the Mexican States, with several flourishing cities.

It was hard to be interested in these things, when all the landscape was wrapped in one dismal blanket of dust, and when every one was tired and uncomfortable. All they could do was to keep their discomforts to themselves, abstain from grumbling, and silently endure to the end. The long day came to a close; it grew dark, lamps were lighted. Steadily they swept onward, and at last, the cheering news was circulated that they were approaching the capital.

The arrival was all as commonplace as possible. No trace of the Montezumas was to be sought in the large modern station, lighted with electric lamps. Jules, from the Café Anglais, came into the car, having recognized Tom on the platform, and taking possession of the party with one swoop, bore them off to carriages, waiting in obedience to a telegram Tom had sent. Three cabs were required to contain them all, and their various wraps, huddled in together in a somewhat promiscuous fashion. They drove off through broad, well-lighted streets, splashing over the cobblestone pavement. It was raining hard.

The rattling of wheels made conversation almost impossible, and they were all too tired to talk. Miss Lejeune and Mrs. Johnstone, in a dazed sort of way, stared about them, and suffered themselves to be helped out of the carriage at the door of the hotel, scarcely knowing or wondering where they were. Tom and Bessie had arrived first, and with bustling Jules led the way. They passed through an entrance into the front of a large and noisy restaurant, and then were led up a mysterious narrow winding stairway and along an entry to a row of rooms, into which they were shown. At the head of the stairway, Madame received them, the lady proprietress, and then Monsieur, the proprietor, with profuse French welcomes, and profuse apologies that one of the rooms was an inside room, which would be changed without fault to-morrow.

Nurse, with Helena and the baby, were relegated to this room; Tom took Jack with him.

And so, after a slight supper, and but one glance at a pile of letters, they all betook themselves to their beds. As Miss Augusta looked round her neat chamber, arranged much as it would be in Paris, she could hardly persuade herself that this cosmopolitan, modern hotel was in the very neighborhood, perhaps near the very spot, of the Halls of the Montezumas, in the centre of the Aztec Kingdom. She had, however, been duly warned that absolutely nothing remains of that ancient city; some modern writers even assert that Tenochtitlan, the Aztec capital, was fifteen miles west of the present site. The City of Mexico, now, is a well-built handsome town of three hundred thousand inhabitants; as the houses are not high, and are for the most part built round patios, in the Spanish fashion, the extent of ground covered over is larger than in cities of the same population crowded into closer quarters. The streets are wide and extend beyond the limits of the city in broad paseos or driveways, with a promenade at the side, shaded with fine trees and lined with stone seats.

There are several hotels, and the Iturbide, a large affair, is the most prominent. The Horners had been advised to try the Café Anglais, and Tom and Bessie went there at once. They were soon so pleased with it that they had no desire to change, and before leaving for Orizaba engaged rooms for the whole party on their return. The hotel is not large, so that rooms must be bespoken beforehand.

It was not much after ten o'clock, but Miss Lejeune had gone to bed so immediately, that she was sound asleep, when she was roused by a knock at the door. To her surprise, it was François, the waiter who spoke French, who with a thousand apologies requested an interview. Slipping on her wrapper, she opened the door. "It is the nurse, Madame, and the young girl. They are not quite happy. I think they wish to see you."

Poor Minton! It flashed through Miss Augusta's mind that they had left her rather thoughtlessly, they were all so tired, without even going to look at her room; and she could speak no word of either French or Spanish. Hastily stepping into her slippers, she followed François, the mysterious meaning of the term "inside-room," soon becoming apparent to her.

The Café Anglais, like other Mexican houses, is built round a patio or open square, — but on so large a scale that the space built upon, is wide enough, up one flight, for the row of rooms looking on the street, an entry way, and another row of rooms look upon the patio. These inside rooms have no windows communicating directly with the outside air. They open upon a narrow gallery running round the sides of the patio. Now this patio, in the Café Anglais, is the restaurant on the ground floor; it is filled with little tables, and as it is very popular in the evening, these tables are all occupied by a lively chattering crowd, who smoke, moreover, the moment they are done eating. The fumes of food, the scent of tobacco, the clattering of dishes, the laughter of guests, the commanding voice of the head waiter, rise to the top of the whole building, for the restaurant is lighted, and, though shut in by glass, ventilated, from above. It may be guessed that the din and odors pause on their way to invade the "inside-room" whose chief light and ventilation come through the doorway opening upon the corridor which overlooks the restaurant below.

The tired nurse put the baby to bed, and Helena also, at a moment when there was a lull in the noise below-stairs, while the guests were quietly taking their soup; but later as the evening advanced, and the fray became furious, the baby woke up and screamed. Helena awoke, and, frightened at the strange situation, fell to crying too. Poor Minton, indeed, did her best to quiet both, but Helena screamed, "I can't stay here! take me away, take me away!" There was an electric bell in the room, but Minton did not know it, or if she had, might not have known how to use it. By and by, however, the screams of the two children triumphed over the racket below, and François, hearing it, ran up of his own accord to find out what was the matter. The nurse could not tell him anything, but his own judgment led him to go and knock at random at one of the doors belonging to the American party, and it happened to be Miss Lejeune's.

She soothed Helena, appeased the nurse, and tried to quiet the baby, though this last was not in her line. Luckily silence had begun to settle on the restaurant, the lights were out, the guests were going. The baby went suddenly to sleep, and Miss Augusta carried Helena off to her room.

The next morning, when the affair became spread abroad, the regrets and apologies of the authorities were most profuse. A room was to be found for Minton, whatever happened; but Mrs. Johnstone at once decided to take nurse and baby into her room, and Bessie invited Helena to share hers and occupy her second bed. The outer rooms are all charming, with large windows looking upon one of two streets, for the hotel is on a corner. After all, it is the charm as well as the fault of the Café Anglais that it is so small. The moderate number of people it will accommodate enjoy the quiet of a small establishment, and the comfort of good service and plenty of attention. Miss Lejeune, however, will warn all travellers against the "inside rooms."

CHAPTER XI.

JUDAS.

IT was Holy week, and our party arrived in Mexico Thursday evening. The next day, therefore, was Good Friday, celebrated there as a day of great rejoicing. All the world was in the street; the shops were shut, but the edge of the sidewalks was crowded with little booths where all sorts of amusing little cheap things were sold, by native women squatting upon the ground, displaying their wares. Mexico is a great place for children's toys; the simple descendants of the Aztecs love to imitate, on a small scale, every thing they use. The native pottery is very pretty, warm in color, and graceful in form, and every possible pot, pan or jug made for common use is reproduced in little, the toy pots, pans and jugs ornamented with just as much care as the large ones.

Especially is Good Friday the day of the children. It is the day of Judas Iscariot, and he is so celebrated on this day, that he might be called the Patron Saint of it, although the whole object of the celebration is to heap him with dishonor and derision. The streets are crowded with people either buying or selling hideous grotesque images called Judases, most of them stuffed with gunpowder so that they can be set off as fireworks. Over the heads of the crowd appear bunches of these figures suspended from a long pole carried along by the vendor. These figures are life-size, or larger than life, made in all sorts of different ways, some on wicker frames, dressed in jacket and trousers of tissue paper, purple, yellow, and pink, with rudely colored faces like big rag-dolls. There are Mrs. Judases with flaunting skirts and bonnets. These big ones are hung by their purchasers on ropes stretched across the streets, from second story balconies, high enough to be out of the way of passengers in the street. They were scattered all over the town, but centred chiefly in the neighborhood of the Zocolo or public square in front of the Cathedral. One was hung over the meeting of the two streets on the corner of which is the Café Anglais. This Judas had on an old straw hat; he was hung about with small loaves of bread, and he wore a paper on his breast which said in Spanish:

"Adieu, friends. I am about to die for my sins," etc., etc.

Besides the large ones there are others a foot or more high, made of papier-maché, in grotesque forms, like fiends, red, with green wings, big heads and hideous expressions, or black, spotted with red and white, with curling tails. Smaller ones are more carefully finished and more absurd; there are even little charms for the watch chain of silver, always in the form of Judas, or, as the man who sold one said, "Yes, devil, yes, Judas, same thing."

Then there are toys,—one of which every child must have in his hand, and every other grown person,—toys which swing round like a watchman's rattle and make the same clacking noise. This is called grinding the bones of Judas,—and the whole town resounds with the sound from the beginning to the end of the festival. The toy consists of a handle, a ratchet, and a wing to swing round, and this wing is ornamented with every imaginable object,— a bouquet of flowers, a sauce-pan, a butterfly, a bird, a wheel-barrow, a chest of drawers, a cannon, a strawberry. There are little wooden carts, such as all children like, the wheels of which grind the bones of Judas. The highest joy of a small boy is to draw one of these carts along the paths of the Zocolo, with a high-colored Judas sitting up in the end of it, and a few minor Judases around him. The boy must be grinding the bones with one hand, and from the other, in the intervals of drawing his cart, he must be taking bites of sugared banana or some form of gingerbread; for there are stalls to furnish these articles in great variety and profusion.

A bewildering scene. The gayly dressed crowds swarm over the streets, sidewalk and roadway alike. Cabs are surrounded, almost submerged by them; here and there a private carriage with impatient horses, forces a way through the mass. The street-cars cut a furrow through the dense crowd, which falls to one side and the other to let the slow mule, and patient smiling Indian driver, draw the rumbling vehicle along; behind it for a moment is left a wake, soon filled up again by the surging, good-natured body of holiday-makers. One especial centre of such an assemblage was in a side street not far away from the Cathedral and Zocolo, for overhead were hung no less than three great Judases, and the people below were amusing themselves throwing up missiles, and shouting with equal joy whether the victim were hit or missed. One of these was a Mrs. Judas, and another was a sort of dude, clothed in solemn black, with tall shirt collar. They were all stuffed full of gunpowder. Bessie found herself in the very thick of the crowd, with little Helena holding her tightly by the hand, but neither was afraid, for the Mexicans about them were gentle and not in the least rough. Their voices were pleasantly modulated, and their shouts of laughter and yells of derision had nothing fierce or violent about them.

At ten o'clock every bell in every church began to ring. Those in the belfries of the Cathedral rang out a merry, clanging peal. This was the signal for setting off the fireworks in the Judases. Smoke issued from the boots of the dude, and one of his legs went off like a pistol. Mrs. Judas's tissue petticoat was in flames, the other figure for a long time hung in a helpless manner swinging from side to side, until the sticks and stones hurled at it from below started it off, and it burst like a rocket.

Bessie took advantage of a coming car to follow in its empty wake, and thus escaped much pushing and hustling. The sight was soon over, and people betook themselves to their homes and hotels.

The next day not a Judas was to be seen or heard of in the whole town. Miss Lejeune wanted another of the little silver devils, but there was no trace of them to be found in shop or booth. The whole supply, the entire subject, was exhausted till next year.

On Saturday, the wife and daughter of the United States Minister

THE VIGA.

called, to return the cards which Tom and Bessie Horner had left on their first arrival. These ladies were most agreeable and pleasant, only regretting that their approaching departure from Mexico made it impossible to see much of the tourists. They were just breaking up their establishment to go home.

The Horners were full of the Judas festivities; their visitors finding them so much interested told them about the other amusements that succeed Lent in Mexico. "You should have been here last week," they said, "for the flower festival of 'Viernes de Dolores,' — the Friday before Good Friday. At sunrise the causeway along the Viga Canal was gay with carriages full of ladies, and gentlemen on horseback, coming and going; and really the show was worth seeing. Booths of evergreen were set up along the bank of the canal, and all the week bands were playing there every forenoon."

From the early time of the Aztecs, the Mexicans have retained their fondness for flowers, which play a prominent part in all their festivals. This occasion is a sort of May-day, or celebration of Spring. Fragrant heaps of flowers were everywhere, and the Indian girls wove garlands or crowns of carnations, poppies, bluets, for their heads; they were most picturesque, with brown skin, flashing black eyes and white teeth, and two long braids of black hair hanging behind, with the universal *rebozo* thrown over their heads and around their shoulders. The broad avenue bordered by trees was crowded with every kind of vehicle, and on the canal were hundreds of canoes large and small, filled with wreath-crowned girls, merry parties of foreigners, Spaniards strumming guitars. At the booths, cooling drinks were sold, as in Spain; of the Mexican love of color even their beverages partake; a bright-colored liquid is always conspicuous on the counters; sometimes with bands of different colors in the same tumblers, and jugs, shelves, awnings are decorated with flowers, trailing green interspersed with sweet-peas, poppies and carnations stuck about everywhere.

The Horners did not fail to see something of this, for the flower decorating is universal, but they wished they had been in time for the gala-day on the Viga.

Easter Sunday passed quietly for our party, reading and writing at the hotel, and Monday Miss Lejeune was busy with Mrs. Johnstone in some additional shopping for things not thought of before her departure, which she thought would be useful in Yucatan. The shops of Mexico are very good, and several have a truly Parisian air. Anything can be bought there, at somewhat irregular prices; some things unreasonably dear, others agreeably cheap. The fun of shopping is away from these grand establishments, under the *Portales*, or arcades, where native vendors, at little booths, or even spread upon the ground, display all sorts of wonders, new and old, at no fixed prices, or rather at prices so absurd, that they are made to be lowered. The chaffing and bargaining required by such a system, is an equal joy to seller and buyer. It reminded Bessie of shopping in Cairo.

Several of the streets are built with the second stories overhanging the street, so that the sidewalks run under them. This gives a passageway sheltered alike from sun and rain, like the arcades of Berne and some other European towns.

On Monday evening, our party were sitting round a moderateur lamp, in Mrs. Johnstone's room, which, being the largest, a corner one, was adopted for their parlor, chatting, knitting, Bessie pretending to read, but constantly joining in the conversation, when there was a tap at the door. "Did anybody ring?" asked Bessie. "Come in!" Nobody ever hears "come in!" through the thick door, so Bessie rose as usual to open it. A tall gentleman in a pith-hat stood before her.

She uttered an exclamation, and stood aside to let him enter. It was Mr. Johnstone.

Bessie was afraid Mrs. Johnstone would faint or have hysterics or something of the sort, but she took it more calmly than might have been expected. In fact, there had been no moment when she was not thinking her husband might arrive, while Bessie on the other hand, to tell the truth, had forgotten all about him. But Miss Lejeune had not. She had been calculating very closely the time he might arrive. When he left the steamer at Yucatan, he was wholly uncertain how long he might be detained there. He was to follow on in some ship of the same line, one of which touches at Progreso, and arrives three days later at Vera Cruz,

THE ABBEY, CAEN.

once a week. It seemed not likely that he could get through at Merida in less than a fortnight, but here he was in a week.

Of course he was received all round most warmly, and his explanations made it all simple.

"There was really nothing much to do in Merida, I found," he said. "I just took the house of my predecessor off his hands, as he was very thankful to have me. I think, Marianne, you will find it perfectly satisfactory in every respect, and I was very much pleased with the place. Merida is a town of over fifty thousand inhabitants, with a theatre, public library, cathedral; I think, Jack, my boy, we shall enjoy life very much."

Jack was perched upon his father's knee with his eyes wide open to prevent falling to sleep, for it was long past his bedtime.

"But Monday night!" said Miss Lejeune, "I don't see how you reached here Monday night!"

"It was a great piece of luck," said Mr. Johnstone. "We had a marvellous run from Campeche, and were in Sunday night. By 'official' magic, I had myself put ashore that evening, and was off by this morning's train."

"Did you have a perfectly horrible journey across the plains up here?" asked Bessie.

"On the contrary, it was delightful," he replied. "How superb the view is of the two volcanoes!"

"Yes; if you only see them," said Bessie, and Mrs. Johnstone added in a dejected tone, "We did not see the first sign of them. I do not believe there are any."

Upon this they all separated for the night, Miss Lejeune well satisfied; for the arrival of Mr. Johnstone seemed to her like the end of her self-appointed mission. "I shall now hand over to him the portfolio," she said to herself.

CHAPTER XII.

RELEASED.

MR. JOHNSTONE'S arrival made everything smooth. Miss Lejeune felt that Tom especially, and Bessie also, would grow restive if they had to stay long in the City of Mexico, before they had seen many other places; for their time was short, or rather they thought it was short. The rainy season begins somewhere about the end of May or first of June; and travellers from "the States" are under the impression that as soon as the rains begin they had better be going northward. The constant rains, however, have a wonderful effect upon the landscape, which grows more beautiful after every shower, and it is the opinion of residents on the table-land of Mexico, that August is the most agreeable month in the year. Then, the daily rains have brought all verdure to perfection, and the land is a bower of green and bloom. The rains cease in October; through the months of a Northern winter the trees in Mexico retain their foliage, and the temperature is mild. Flowers keep on blossoming in the open air, but, without rain, the aspect of things grows gradually parched, so that by April the fields have the dried-up look that New England hillsides show in September after a long dry summer. Spring, therefore, in Mexico, answers in one sense to the Northern autumn, and although it seems summer-like enough to people who have just left a few inches of snow and sleet, the land is really waiting for its yearly renewal, which comes soon in the form of refreshing rain; the old leaves at once give place to new ones, without any interval of bare branches. The arid plains are covered with innumerable bright flowers, and even the maguey, whose great stiff leaves look as if they were cut out of tin and painted with Paris green, put out tender leaves. The Northern winter is the time naturally chosen for visiting Mexico, for travellers from the North wish to avoid their own disagreeable season, but the Horners were led to wish they could see the country in all its midsummer bloom. They were pledged to come home not long after the first of May, and wished to make hay while the sun shone.

"Tom," said Bessie, tapping at his door the next morning, "can't you come in and have coffee with us? We want to confer."

"All right!" he answered, out of a very sound morning nap. "Order it for three, — and eggs!" he called after her.

"Tom," said Miss Augusta, ten minutes later, while François was arranging three big cups on the table, and pouring out streams of *café con leche*, "we can be off now for Morelia as soon as you like."

"Will the Johnstones go with us?" asked Tom.

"O no," she answered quickly. "You know we cannot be carting that baby about any longer."

"The nurse appears to be a drivelling idiot," remarked Tom quietly, as he tapped the top of his egg.

"O, no, she is all very well," said Miss Lejeune, "although she has not the command of more than a dozen languages; but so big a party is troublesome, and Mrs. Johnstone really does not care for travelling. They will stay here, I think, some little time."

"I should not mind having Jack with us," said Tom.

"We might take Helena," suggested Bessie.

"If only to prove once more your family resemblance to your father," said Miss Lejeune, laughing.

Mr. Horner had, more than once, proposed similar outside additions to the travelling party.

"Do not think of it, if it bores you, aunt Dut," said Tom.

"Not at all, my dear," she replied. "If the parents mean to stay here a week or so, they would be glad to be relieved of the children, and we could bring them back in time for them to go to Merida."

"Well, then, why do not we go to day?" said Tom. "I long to be out of this, and we can go as far as Toluca."

"The wash! the wash!" cried Bessie.

But after all, this exceptional set of people decided to go without their wash, which had been given out a couple of days before. Mrs. Johnstone agreed to take charge of it with hers. The parents gladly consented to the plan for Jack and Helena, who of course were overjoyed.

"I shall have to be here at least a fortnight," said Mr. Johnstone, "waiting for letters, and also on account of some business at the British Consulate; so do not hurry yourselves in the least, but return me my children when you have done with them, that's all."

So after a somewhat hastened lunch, the party were off with portmanteaus and straps piled in about them, to the station of the National railway. They left their large trunks at the Café Anglais, being sure to return there. In Mexico, one can do with very little luggage, for the climate is so even, the same clothes answer day after day. A warm wrap, and a moderately light travelling-dress are necessary. Miss Lejeune found it a good plan to have a black silk on hand, and advised Bessie to do so.

It is but lately that railroads have made travelling easy throughout Mexico, and only since 1880 that the lines were begun which have already opened new fields to the traveller, and which, in the future, will reveal still more interesting regions for historical and archæological students, or for the pursuit of the picturesque.

The Mexican National Railway is built in pursuance of a decree of the Mexican Congress, which contracted for the construction of a railway and telegraph line from the City of Mexico to the

Pacific Ocean at the port of Manzanillo; also a line and telegraph, from Mexico to the northern frontier, at Laredo. The line was begun in 1880, at both ends. It is in operation from the capital to San Miguel, on its way towards the States, and from Laredo, in the north, where it connects with the Texas Mexican Railway, it is completed as far as Saltillo in a southerly direction. From these points the two ways stretch out their longing hands to each other, and slowly advance to a meeting which will take place when the stability of the Mexican government is equal to the ardor of Yankee enterprise. The Mexican Central Railroad has a through line to the States.

Meanwhile, the western branch of the National is in operation as far as Morelia, the capital of Michoacan, on its way towards the Pacific. The cities made accessible by these lines, were formerly to be reached only by diligence, on the roughest of roads. It is moreover only within a few years that travelling has been at all safe in Mexico, on account of brigands and robbers who infested the mountain-passes, and carried on matters in their own way. A liberal government, wisely encouraging the civilizing influence of railroad construction, has done away with such dangers, and travelling in Mexico is now as safe as anywhere else. Travellers' tales of bold robberies in diligences still float in the air, but these may safely now be considered as tales of the past. Laying a railroad over unfrequented country is like opening a strong draught of air through some dark cave. Cobwebs and crimes disappear at the sound of an engine whistle. Banditti and locomotives do not belong together, any more than the helmet of Don Quixote matches a Colt's revolver.

We may regret the picturesque element of the old régime, but it is more comfortable to arrive safely at one's journey's end, with luggage all safe and a good supper waiting, than to alight from a diligence in a robbed and bleeding condition, to be obliged to borrow clothing, and go to bed hungry.

So the Horners started cheerfully from the Colonia Station in the comfortable first-class car of the National Railway, and did not repine at being whirled out of the city by a snorting engine rather than a set of merry mules with jangling bells. The National is built on the narrow gauge, and the cars are narrower than usual, so that the party seemed at first somewhat squeezed together; but there is really plenty of room in a seat for two persons. As they passed out of town, Chapultepec with its white walls was to be seen on the left, and the scenery soon became magnificent looking backward into the valley of Mexico, as they slowly ascended a rising grade. There was a last glimpse of the city just before the train rushed into a tunnel six hundred feet long.

CHAPTER XIII.

TOLUCA.

TOM had arrived in Mexico armed with letters of introduction to some of the gentlemen connected with the National Road, and to them he owed a great deal of kindness and good advice in making his plans. Thus he learned that it was by all means desirable to go to Morelia, as a city of great attraction, and his friend Mr. Purdy advised him to make the journey a long one, by stopping at Toluca for the first night.

As soon as they were off, Tom introduced himself and the ladies to the conductor of the train, an American, just as proud of the railroad and glad to show it off, as he was of his nice little son, whom they saw the next day. He brought camp-stools for the party to sit on the back platform and see the narrow ribbon of the road winding through difficult cuts, creeping along the edges of steep slopes, and crossing leisurely slender-looking trestle-work to the *Cima*, or summit, over ten thousand feet above sea-level; then they began to descend; the scenery was fine, the near hills brown and sere, dotted with evergreens, snow-capped peaks appearing against the sky.

"You see, Jack," said Tom, "the valley of Mexico is something like a great flat tin pan. If we want to come out we must climb up the inside and come down the outside."

"Or else make a hole through, near the bottom," said Jack.

"And I should think," said Helena, who had rather a squeaky voice, "the tin was rather thick to cut through." She had the long tunnel still in her mind.

"It will be dark when we come to Toluca," said the conductor, "and you had better keep pretty close to your baggage. There will be plenty of fellows there to take it."

"Helena, you come with me," said Bessie, "and Jack, stick to Tom."

It was nearly nine o'clock, and dark, when the train stopped. An army of *cargadores* came into the car for their things, and each secured one for himself. Miss Lejeune made sure of a small boy about twelve years old, who manfully grasped her big valise in one hand, her shawl strap in the other, and wanted to relieve her of a bunch of umbrellas. She followed him close along the platform, passing through the crowd which beset it, as usual. At the end, in a broad open space, stood a row of tram-cars, with lights. Miss Augusta arrived first; soon came Bessie with her *cargador* carrying her luggage and Helena's, and Helena herself fast by the hand. Last came Tom with his, then the car filled up, and they jogged off to the town.

The hotel was an immense great place, built around a huge stone-paved patio. It was very dark, not lighted at all, in fact, and as there was some confusion about the rooms which had been telegraphed for, the party for a time seemed to be hopelessly walking round and round the corridor above the patio, surrounded by a swarm of brown *muchachos* in white garments, all talking and advising in Spanish, carrying a few vague candles, and loaded with valises and rugs.

Finally rooms enough were found, and all was settled, the children who had been amply fed at way stations put to bed, while the others went below for some supper. This was the first time in Mexico they were thrown on their own Spanish resources, for at Orizaba they had used the easier French. As it was the first time too that the two Horners were alone with Miss Lejeune, they all enjoyed the freedom of their old long intimacy.

In the morning they found Toluca very pretty, and wished they could stay there longer. It is the capital of the State of Mexico, and its valley among the highlands, is the highest inhabited land in the country, with a cold climate, which makes the city a favorite summer resort; it stands at the elevation of something like eight thousand six hundred feet.

When Bessie awoke, she found the sounds of music which had been mixed up with her dreams were real, coming from a band somewhere below. From her window, at the side of the hotel, she saw the snow-covered peak of the Nevada de Toluca, with a little church on the side of it. This is the fourth peak in height in Mexico, — over fifteen thousand feet. It was visible all that morning, as they pursued their way westward. They were off and in the train again at half-past nine, and rode and rode until nine in the evening, a long day and fatiguing, although the scenery was fine, going downward now all the way, leaving evergreens on the desolate upper-lands for the richer vegetation of the lower region. The route leads through the valley of the River Lerma, which was sometimes close to them with huge tree-trunks standing in the water like great elephants. An excellent *almuerzo* at Flor de Maria gave them courage for the day. At Acambaro, which they reached about four in the afternoon, the northern line of the railway leaves the western branch, going to Celaya on its way to join, when completed, the great route to the States. They went on to Morelia, passing just at sunset Lake Cuitzao, eighteen miles long, for a good part of which it is close to the track. It was covered with flocks of birds, hovering over its surface, and ducks floating upon it, and Tom learned that the shooting there was capital. There ought to have been a superb sunset effect, but alas! a searching wind arose before evening which filled the air with thick clouds of dust, not quite so bad as that on the plains as they were approaching Mexico, but enough to hide the view, and the sky was leaden and lowering. The children had been told to look out for rose-colored flamingoes on the lake, and had their eyes glued to the window for that purpose, but no flamingoes nor anything else rose-colored was visible. It was disappointing, and they became tired and cross. It may be feared that the grown-up people were also; they grew silent, and longed for the journey to be over.

But Tom said, "We must see more of that lake. What a pity there is no good place to stop at, so we could go out on it."

"The sketching must be lovely," said Miss Lejeune in rather a sleepy voice. "When did you say we shall reach Morelia?"

It was nine o'clock, and after dark. The same game of *cargadores* was played at the station; the same scene in the tram-car. At the hotel everything was ready for them, and they were enchanted with the looks of it.

"Is it not curious?" said Miss Augusta, whose spirits always rose at sight of a new hotel, for some reason or other. "Although these inns have all a general similarity, each one we come to is entirely different from any of the rest. I think I shall like this one the best."

"You dear old Dut!" said Bessie. "You always like the last the best, you know you do."

The next morning showed them that the hotel was on a long straight street, the principal one of the town, traversed as usual by the track of the street cars. From the balconies the vista either way was pretty. Beyond the cathedral on the left, the long street stretched towards the station. On the right the pretty church of Santa Catalina appeared, and in the extreme distance were the arches of the aqueduct, and the trees of the Alameda. A funny thing, which they first noticed in Morelia, was the long tin or earthen spouts projecting from the houses just below the flat roof. When it rains, the water comes pouring out of these spouts down into the very middle of the street, where an open gutter receives it and carries it off. Thus passers on the sidewalk are unharmed by dripping from the roofs, while a regular shower-bath falls into the roadway. The tram-way is on one side of the central gutter,

LAKE CUITZIO.

to which the cobble-stone road slightly slopes from each sidewalk. It is a simple sewerage which seems to answer fairly well.

The Morelia houses are seldom more than two stories high; the one on the street is occupied by shops for the most part, while the people live on the stage above. The lower story is so high that the balconies of the second one are well up over the street, which to any one who cares for such things, is an endless source of amusement. Not many carriages pass, but at regular intervals the street car jogs by, drawn by one mule. Then came a group of donkeys laden with fodder, perhaps a little donkey trotting beside his mamma, a man carrying a huge sofa covered with crimson reps, a devotee going to church in her black lace mantilla with fan and prayer book, a small boy selling cakes which he carries on his head spread out upon a board. Watching such sights fills up so well an idle hour, that the idle hour may become two, or more, without a change of occupation. Although the street is so quiet that there is a tinge of green between the cobble-stones, Morelia is a stirring place, and, since the building of the railroad, promises to become more so. It is the capital of its State, has over twenty-five thousand inhabitants and considerable trade. Cotton and woollen, candles and tobacco, are manufactured there. A huge hotel is in process of construction, upon the site of an old church, which promises to be very attractive, as it stands on a corner of the principal street looking upon the Plaza de la Paz, and across that to the Cathedral. The hotel where the Horners were was kept by a German. It was attractive on account of its neatness and quiet. There was no restaurant in the house, which was merely a collection of rooms built round a patio. It had once been a convent, and Bessie could imagine that within its solid stone walls nuns had told their beads, and pined away, perhaps, with broken hearts, according to the conventional standard.

Their rooms were very large and very high, and the walls were two feet thick. The great windows opened, casement-fashion, against these thick walls, and might stand open day and night, so mild was the temperature. Each room had its one window and little balcony, and opposite the window was the door opening upon the corridor, round two sides of the patio. This corridor was pleasant to sit upon, for the courtyard was open to the bright blue sky; a light railing ran around it, and light iron columns supported its roof. These must have been modern, and how the nuns went in and out of their cells before the corridor was built, Bessie never knew. A great banana-tree, an ash, and an evergreen grew up tall from below.

CHAPTER XIV.

ANAHUAC.

ANAHUAC, which means "by the water," was the ancient name for the Valley of Mexico, the great tract of land at an elevation of more than seven thousand feet from the ocean. At first the name was applied only to the vicinity of the several lakes which are found in the neighborhood, but later it came to be applied to all the regions which after the conquest formed New Spain.

Before the conquest there were different tribes inhabiting Anahuac, speaking different dialects, of which the leading one was the Mexican, which was rich, polished and expressive. The history of these early tribes is obscure and uncertain; it is generally assumed that the first people came from Asia, entering North America by Behring's Straits.

Traditions of the people found by the Spaniards described the first inhabitants of Anahuac as men extremely tall, living in the neighborhood of Tlascala and Cholula. They were rough and savage, lived by hunting with bow and arrow, and devoured their game raw. They were agile, fierce and brave. The tradition relates that this race of giants was destroyed by a later tribe who came from the North and exterminated them, afterwards occupying their territory. But the giants, according to this, left monuments, evidently the work of a numerous people under some kind of intelligent rule.

The *Mayas*, another tribe, are supposed to have crossed Anahuac, coming from the North to plant an advanced civilization in Yucatan several centuries before the Christian Era. It was the traces of their early work which Mr. Johnstone hoped to investigate during his stay in Merida. Of the successive tribes supposed to have migrated from the North, the Toltecs are the first of whom there is certain information as advanced in arts and civilization. These came from the north of Anahuac, and afterwards founded the city of Tollan, now Tula, sometime in the latter half of the seventh century. There are still some ruins of their buildings on the hills around Tula, and some of their sculpture is preserved in the town. They were a worthy people; not warlike, and inclined to the virtues of truthfulness and honesty; clean, industrious, devout. They flourished for four centuries under an absolute monarchy, and extended their kingdom in every direction.

QUETZALCOATL.

All these people who came from the North are spoken of as Nahuas, speaking a language called Nahuatl, as they have evidently a common origin, although different sets migrated at long intervals, one after the other.

In 987, it is said, came to the Toltec throne Tecpancaltzin, the eighth sovereign. At this time the kingdom had reached its greatest splendor, reaching as far as Toluca, where there was a magnificent palace of stone, with walls decorated with hieroglyphics recording historical events. In the end of this reign appeared Quetzalcoatl, "the feathered serpent," a mysterious personage, white and bearded, who is often mentioned in the early traditions of Anahuac.

The eighth king of the Toltecs married Xochitl, and the legend says it was because she offered him to drink honey extracted from the maguey. If she was the person who first invented this beverage, she has much to answer for.

Their son, Meconetzin, or "child of maguey," reigned after his father. He ruled at first with prudence, but afterwards became a vicious tyrant. This may have been the result of the drink invented by his mother. The kingdom declined, and fell to pieces in the most disastrous manner, in consequence of famine, pests, and invasions.

The Toltecs seem to have been dispersed about 1100, after a reign of four centuries, to us vague and legendary. They were followed by the *Chichimecs*, a savage, brave people, who came from the North, like the rest, and established themselves in the Toltec cities spreading towards the Gulf of Mexico. Their power lasted until it was overthrown by an alliance of three tribes, the Aztecs, Acolhuas, and Tepanecs, in 1541. The Tepanecs had come from the North, a long time before, but these were not the Mexicans of Montezuma. The Chichimecs had their capital at Tezcoco, at the eastern end of the great salt lake, the largest of the lakes of Anahuac. During the period of this Chichimec dynasty, the Mexicans or Aztecs came and founded their city of Tenochtitlan, which is now Mexico.

"And I will tell you about them another time," said Bessie, who was expounding these historic fragments according to her wont to the children, while the others, as it happened, were listening.

"Has she not got it all down fine?" asked Tom of Jack in a low tone.

"Slang again, Tom," said Bessie reprovingly. "You know Mrs. Johnstone especially wants to improve Jack's English."

"Well, go on about your Chichimecs," said Tom.

"They seem to have allowed the new tribe to come and settle at Tenochtitlan, in fact the Mexicans were but poor things at that time. The Chichimecs had good kings, and kept their realm in good order, but as time went on they were troubled by wars with the neighboring tribes. In one of these struggles, the Mexicans, who had grown strong, helped the Chichimecs to shake off the tyrant Maxtla, and put the lawful heir to the throne on it; his name was Nezahualcoyotl. He changed his title to King of Acolhuacan, and the kingdom kept this last name until it fell at the Spanish conquest.

"This king with the long name that begins with Nez, was one of the most notable of the old history of Anahuac. Perhaps his youth, spent in adversity, while the tyrant Maxtla usurped his father's throne, had a good effect upon him. Unlike the barbarous creed of the Mexicans, he believed in one unknown God, the author of the universe, of which the proof exists in hymns written by him in praise of his Maker. He was a brave warrior, and a great ruler, law-maker, philosopher and poet. He died in 1472.

"The year Isabella of Spain was twenty-one years old," continued Bessie, interrupting herself.

"Only think," said Miss Lejeune, "how little she dreamed of this great wise king writing poems in a country which would later on belong to her family!"

"His son Nezahualpilli, the tenth monarch of Acolhuacan, was also good and wise. He reigned a long time, which brings us along towards the period of the conquest. His sons at first quarrelled and then divided the kingdom, north and south, between them. These divisions, which were common among the early kings of Anahuac, were unwise for them, and lucky for Cortés, who had the skill to set one petty king against the others, sure to take the advantage for himself. During the separate reign of these two brothers, came the news of Cortés's arrival in the country with his army. They at once concluded, as almost all the people of Anahuac did, that these warriors were the white men with beards who were, according to tradition, to come some day from the East, and they resolved to receive them peacefully. Ixtlilxochitl, one of the brothers, went so far as to send emissaries to Cortés inviting him to his part of the kingdom. The other brother, Cacamatzin, became indignant later at the treatment by Cortés of Montezuma, who was his uncle, by the way, and began to raise an army to resist the Spaniards, but he fell into the hands of Cortés, was imprisoned, and afterwards killed in his presence. Ixtlilxochitl, on the other hand, who remained friendly to Cortés, was allowed later by him to call himself king of Acohuacan. He was baptized a Christian, adopting the name of Ferdinand; he accompanied Cortés on several of his military expeditions. He was the last sovereign of the dynasty founded four centuries previous, by the Chichimec king, Xolotl.

"Now," said Bessie, "I want you to see how there were different kingdoms here at and before the time of the conquest, and that it was not all Mexico, by any means. There was, besides these countries settled close around the lakes, the ancient kingdom of Michoacan, a part of which is the present State of Michoacan, and that is where we are now. The old kingdom included the modern States, Jalisco and Colima ; that is, it stretched away down to the Pacific Ocean. The Michhuacas, or Tarascos, who formally ruled here, are supposed to be more modern than the Toltecs, and the others I have been telling about, but they were ancient enough. The kingdom flourished side by side with the Mexican ; the last Aztec king, after Montezuma, who bravely resisted Cortés till the very last, sent ambassadors to Michoacan proposing an alliance against the common enemy. All the efforts of this brave king were in vain. The Mexican kingdom had to fall before the power of the Spaniards, and the news of this triumph, so great and so final, was followed by the submission of Michoacan, and many other places. But there was trouble with the natives later; in the time of Mendoza, the first Spanish viceroy, the Indians of Jalisco had to be put down, and it was in an encounter with them that Alvarado, the famous companion of Cortés, was killed.

"Mendoza, during his rule in New Spain, founded two cities in Michoacan, one was Guadelajara, up in the north of it, and the other was Morelia; but he named it Valladolid, after his own birthplace in Spain. The royal parchment exists, sent by the queen Juana, under date of October 27th, 1537, in which permission is given to the viceroy, 'as he has found or discovered a suitable place in the Province of Michoacan, to start a city there with more than sixty Spanish families and nine priests.'

"Mendoza selected the site when he was travelling off to pacify the revolted inhabitants of Jalisco; and on his return a great ceremonial of foundation took place. All the people from round about were assembled, the royal mandate was read aloud, the commissioners and governors of the Indians kissed the parchment, and mass was performed before an altar erected under the branches of trees. Then followed a great feast which lasted three days, the land was divided into estates and public squares, and the estates were given to the 'more than sixty families.'

"So that was the beginning of Morelia, or rather of Valladolid," said Bessie, "as Mendoza wished it to be called."

"What a pity they have changed the name!" said Tom.

"Why did they?" asked inquiring Jack.

"In honor of a patriot who was born here,—José Morelos, in 1765; he was one of the Heroes of Independence, and they changed the name of the town after the Republic was established, in 1828, not so very long ago."

CHAPTER XV.

MORELIA.

ONE of the rooms in the hotel at Morelia was a huge double one, with two windows, two little iron beds in the corners, one each side of the double door. It was scantily furnished in comparison with Miss Lejeune's rooms in New York, full of knickknacks, small tables, low chairs and footstools; but there was as much furniture as travellers require. A good-sized round table in the centre left ample space for two huge *balançoires*, rockingchairs of bamboo; a great wardrobe stood against one side of the room, and there were two washstands with a looking-glass on each. Bessie took this room with little Helena, whom she chose to regard as her special charge, and Miss Lejeune had the single room adjoining, which connected with the large one by a door. The convent walls were so thick that no sound transpired from one room to the other. Tom and Jack had another room further along on the corridor. As at Orizaba, the family often found themselves on their separate balconies looking down into the street, where indeed they spent much time.

In the morning, coffee was brought from the restaurant by a brown *muchacho* in white garments, his black hair sticking up from his forehead like the broom called a Turk's head. This is the prevailing fashion among the descendants of the Aztecs. Probably, as their hair will not grow down, they let it grow up.

He brought the tray through the streets on his shoulder, and came back for it later; as every one was ready for it, it was served on the round table in the big room, which was adopted for the family sitting-room. Afterwards the sad Pedro removed the tray, made the beds, mopped up the floor, and put the rooms in order.

Pedro was the only servant attached to the premises. He was a melancholy elderly Mexican with a faded air of decayed gentility about his very rusty garments, which were of ancient broadcloth, descended to him from his master. His speech was Spanish of an obscure type; that is, it was not always comprehensible to Bessie and Miss Augusta, so that they communicated with him as much as possible by signs. He possessed no retiring-place he could call his own, other than an empty wooden box in the corner of the corridor where he sat to black the shoes, and where he kept some cast-off blossom in a cheap crockery jug. He slept on a piece of matting at the turn of the stairway leading down from the corridor to the street, and was never known to lay aside his day-clothing. When the morning was cool, as it was towards the rainy season, he might be found at dawn, sitting on his box, blacking, or engaged in gloomy contemplation, wrapped close in his thin, ragged serape, with a sombrero on his head. Tom thought him stupid, but he was faithful and watchful, and absolutely devoted. Bessie's imagination invested him with charms that were not all his own.

After coffee, it was the plan, often altered, however, to start for the Alameda. The tram-car passed the hotel at regular intervals. It could be seen far off in the distance, and the cheerful horn of the driver gave warning in ample time to stop it. Its track leads through the principal street to the eastern end of the town, where three broad ways diverge. It passes over the middle one, called the Calzada, to its terminus near a picturesque church surrounded by cypress-trees, old pointed rusty evergreens.

Here is the Alameda, laid out long ago with a certain formality, a *rond-point*, with a stone fountain in the middle, approached by broad alley-ways, defined by a circle of stone seats, overhung by tall ash-trees. The seats are moss-grown; grass grows in the deserted avenues. The shade of the old trees is so thick that stray sunbeams only dance over the pavement. The stones of the fountain are broken; the garden which surrounded the place is overgrown and choked with weeds, but it is crowded with old rosebushes, always blossoming, sweet peas cropping up in the grass, run-out pansies and other flowers.

Tom and Jack discovered this place the first afternoon, and their report of it was so joyful, that the next day the whole party started early for the Alameda, armed with sketching-blocks, to pass the morning. This became their habit, for it was very pretty there. Nurse-maids of Morelian children brought their little charges, but there was always an air of desolated quiet about the spot. Helena made the acquaintance of three little Mexican children, much smaller than herself, with whom she had no power of conversation, as they talked only Spanish. It was amusing to see them all playing together, making gardens in the pathway, and sticking up flowers in them. The invention of the Yankee child amazed the little Mexicans, who saw her laying out miniature Alamedas with silent delight. Beyond and beside the Alameda stretched the large Paseo, also laid out in regular avenues, but so long neglected that the original plan is lost. Broad alley-ways overhung by superb great trees intersect it, the spaces between over-run with flowers. White roses with masses of flowers trail over tumble-down palings near a thatched hut occupied by picturesque Indians; two or three little brown children were often running about in front of the door, while a friendly donkey cropped the grass in the neighborhood, and occasionally filled the air with his cheerful melancholy bray. Why did these people live in the Paseo? *Quien sabe? Quien sabe?* which means "who knows?" is equivalent to "nobody knows," and accompanied by a certain shrug of the shoulders, it implies, "nobody thinks it is worth while to know."

A long, long aqueduct brings water to the city from the hills at the east. Its graceful warm-colored stone arches are seen from the Alameda stretching far into the distance. It crosses the Paseo, and passes over the street at the entrance of the town, where the Calzada begins that leads to the Alameda. This is a broad paved way with continuous stone seats on each side, entirely shaded by large trees. Pleasant houses line it on either side, with glimpses through open doorways to patios, where blossoming vines hang over the corridors, and fountains play.

The Horners found themselves always watching for these open doorways. The walls of the houses are blank, with blinds closed upon the street, but every little while, as the street-car rolls along, comes a glimpse through a passageway of a flood of sunshine and some splendid vine. The one which at the time the Horners were in Mexico was most resplendent, was called there the "Camellina," known to Miss Lejeune in greenhouses by some other name; but never had she seen it in the profusion it reached there. The branches of pink blossoms, or rather flower-leaves, were a yard long, or more, and fell over the green in long festoons.

Climbing roses were there, too, Bignonia, and many other things they did or did not know.

"It is a pretty, pretty town!" exclaimed Miss Lejeune, "I could wander about this Alameda forever."

On another Calzada, not far away from the Alameda, were the *Baños del Recreo*, and it was well to take this recreation on their way back to the hotel.

A friendly woman, mistress of the establishment, sold them tickets at a counter in a little room at the entrance of the baths. Passing through this they came into a little snug garden, and there was a noise of water rushing, and the sounds of merry laughter from the girls' swimming-bath. While their baths were being prepared, they sat in the corridor looking at the flowers, while Tom stole a "ladies' delight" for his buttonhole. Then each retired to his or her little cell for a refreshing plunge in warm or cold water, after which they were ready for a brisk walk home, or to take the street car at the archway.

If they walked, perhaps they stopped to buy a crisp fresh head of lettuce stuck full of bright red poppies, of an old Indian woman who sat on the edge of the sidewalk to sell these and nothing else. She had a rude parasol over her head of matting stretched on sticks, like a boy's kite, and set up on a pole. Bessie longed to take home one of these things, but it would have been an awkward piece of baggage.

Twelve o'clock was the time for *almuerzo;* our party walked from their rooms one or two blocks, under the Portal Hidalgo, and down another street to their restaurant, where, crossing a stone-paved patio, they lunched by themselves in a little room, rather dungeon-like, lighted by a barred window high up from the ground. The table was narrow, and rather high; the chairs were decidedly low. This is a funny Mexican peculiarity; as if the inhabitants liked to have their food close under their chins.

LADIES' DELIGHT.

After that, the hot walk back in the sun,—then delightful well-earned repose, much dawdling on balconies. The afternoons had each its plan for an excursion. It was growing dark always as they went to dinner; before the cathedral flamed torches of the street-vendors of fruit and candy. The fading sunset was before them, and as they came back they often stopped to listen to the band playing in the Zocolo, while the strong scent of datura was wafted over the garden beds.

And so home, and early to bed, after a chat about their round table over the events of the day, if events may be called the incidents of so uneventful a life. It was very happy. The lovely climate, neither too hot nor too cold, the picturesque people, the flowers, so luxuriant even in this autumn of the Mexican year, made up a bundle of pleasures not always found in travelling.

CHAPTER XVI.

MEXICAN CHURCHES.

THE first care of the Spaniards," said Bessie, "after they had conquered Mexico, and of the good priests who came with them, or followed afterwards, was to set up churches everywhere, and appoint bishops for them, so as to convert the natives, and to make the country a Christian land.

"As soon as they had possession of Michoacan, the viceroy Mendoza sent a venerable man as bishop to Tzintzunzan, a primitive old town, to establish the church of Michoacan, and began to build the cathedral there, but they decided to change the place for it to Patzcuaro, near by, the favorite place of recreation of the ancient kings, and a lovely situation, where perhaps we shall go."

"How soon?" asked Jack, starting up as if to make ready at that moment.

"Not now," said Bessie; "we are very well off here, and it is a hard journey to go there. So they began the cathedral at Patzcuaro, which was so magnificent, an old writer says, 'that it entirely satisfies the ideas of every one who remembers it,' and they all say of this great work that it would have been the eighth wonder of the world. But it was never finished, for when Valladolid was founded, they decided to make that the chief town, and to have the cathedral there instead.

"The present cathedral was begun in 1680; it was finished sixty-four years afterwards, as you may see over the porch —

Año de 1744.

A space of time including the end of the reign of Charles the Second in Spain, and the whole of that of Philip the Fifth."

The effect of the cathedral is fine, on account of the lofty well-proportioned towers. It stands in an open space between two plazas, where especially the light of the setting sun falls well upon the façade. There are many bells in the towns, some of them huge. One, the largest, is only heard at rare intervals, on occasions of great importance. The others sound frequently, indeed it seemed as if some bell were ringing pretty much all the time in Morelia, for there are twenty-seven churches, all of which join in the peal from time to time, without any cause the Horners could find out, though doubtless with good reason.

The interior of the cathedral, indeed of the most of the churches, was uninteresting to our travellers after the splendid old cathedrals of Spain. The pictures are but copies or imitations of frescos at Rome, the interior decorations tawdry and tasteless for the most part. It must be remembered that the churches have been denuded of many of the silver screens and statues which once adorned them, for purposes of government.

For the history of the church in Mexico shows a great change from the Spanish conquest to the present time. Cortés was thoroughly in earnest in his wish to convert the natives. He requested the emperor, Charles the Fifth, to send out as priests "godly persons, members of the religious fraternities whose lives might be a fitting commentary on their teaching." As early as 1524, twelve Franciscan friars arrived in New Spain,—learned men of pure lives, who devoted themselves to their sacred cause indifferent to every personal sacrifice. They taught at first through interpreters, but set themselves to learning the native language; they opened schools for the natives, to improve as well as enlighten their minds. The Indians took very kindly to the new treatment. They not only learned to read and write, but entered with zeal into the desire of their teachers to efface the traces of the old religion. After school, an old book says, "one or two brethren used to take the pupils to some neighboring *teocalli*, and by working at it for a few days they levelled it to the ground. In this way they demolished in a short time all the Aztec temples, great and small, so that not a vestige of them remained."

This was a great pity, for so many hieroglyphic manuscripts were destroyed among the idols and temples, that we have lost all these would have told us about the early inhabitants of the country. However, the business of conversion went on rapidly, and at this day the Indians make good Catholics; superstitious, and devoted to the forms of the church. They transferred many of their graceful ceremonials, such as decoration with flowers, to the new religion, where they were not out of place.

The country was becoming peopled with Spaniards and their descendants, a race wholly different from the natives. These, in the course of three hundred years since the conquest, have drifted away from the Spanish type, as much or more than the Yankees have from their Anglo-Saxon ancestors. The Mexicans talk Spanish and derive many of their manners and customs from those of Spain, but distance from the mother-country, difference of climate and the influence of other races, have altered their characters and their habits of thinking. From the time of the conquest until 1821, Mexico belonged to Spain and was governed by viceroys appointed by the Spanish crown. Some of these were good and able men, like Mendoza; but as time went on, everything was made to subserve the interests and profit of the church. The kings and viceroys depended upon the power of the church to control the people, and with so much power the bishops and priests became tyrannical, and used the money and the faith of the people for their own ends. The country was covered with cathedrals, churches, monasteries and convents, but there was no popular educaation; superstition and ignorance were encouraged that the priests might keep the control of the country in their own hands.

In the beginning of this century liberty was in the air; the Mexicans rose against the rule of the Spaniards, and resolved to be free. It is no wonder that with freedom came to them an utter revulsion of feeling toward the church. When they had the power in their own hands, they emptied all the monasteries and nunneries, turned out the monks and nuns, made laws restricting the power of the bishops and priests to almost nothing, and exiled them if they refused to obey, and invited Protestant missionaries to come into the country, promising to protect their rights.

The churches had become immensely rich, owning a great deal of land on which magnificent churches, and grand monasteries and convents were built, and many beautiful statues and silver work, the ornaments of the cathedrals. All these riches the new government took away in their indignation, leaving the churches bare, turning the convents to other purposes, or selling them; this is why so many hotels are now found occupying the old homes of monks and nuns.

Thus while the churches remain, many of them in every town, they are bare of ornament within, and lack the pomp and circumstance of ceremonials, such as the Horners had seen in countries where the government professes to be Catholic.

"That saves a great deal of trouble," said Tom, "for I always did hate going about to see churches."

"Oh! not in Spain, Tom," exclaimed Bessie.

"Well, there the architecture is splendid, and the pictures are master-pieces which cannot be seen anywhere else. But I think, Jack, that you and I shall not trouble the churches of Morelia much."

Bessie was more persevering, and either alone or with little Helena, she penetrated into most of the twenty-seven, sometimes rewarded by finding things which Miss Lejeune approved after they were discovered. Among these was a gold screen in the little

PLAZA SANTO DOMINGO, MEXICO.

church of las Rosas, very rich and handsome, reminding them of similar work in Spain. It looked as if it might have been brought from some more ancient church, and fitted into its present place. Connected with this church was a sort of home for poor women, and a hospital, with a pretty garden full of roses, as usual in Morelia.

The church called Santa Catalina de Sena, with its pretty open belfry and dome, formed an important part of the view from the hotel balconies. Connected with this was formally a convent founded as early as the end of the sixteenth century, in another place. It was transferred to the present one in 1738 with a solemn procession, and there is now existing in the church a great picture representing the occasion. Sometimes there have been sixty or seventy nuns living there; in 1863, when all the convents were broken up by order of government, there were but twenty-eight who had to leave their peaceful retreat with its pretty garden. We cannot but feel compassion for so many poor helpless women suddenly cast adrift upon the world from all the convents of Mexico. There was a brief time later when Maximilian came to be emperor in Mexico, that these women returned to their convent, like wandering sheep to their accustomed fold; but when the republic again triumphed they were again set adrift. Their convent is now occupied by a batalion of federal infantry, and their extensive garden is cut up into house lots.

"What a pity," said Miss Lejeune, "that everything that is picturesque arrests the march of progress. Those poor old nuns enjoying their tranquil life in this lovely climate, tending their roses, did us no harm; what a pity they had to go!"

"They did harm, I believe," said Bessie; "they had the teaching of the children, and they made a point of teaching them to hate the liberal government, and to make all the trouble they could. If the nuns had done nothing but attend to their rosebushes, they might have been here now, instead of that row of soldiers basking in the sun."

"O yes," assented Miss Lejeune, readily changing round as she was apt to do to the opposite side of the subject she had herself started. "I dare say they were a narrow-minded set of obstinate women, and the government were well rid of them."

"Only," said Tom, "they all went somewhere, and I suppose they all continued being actively disagreeable wherever they were."

"Perhaps they are all dead," said Helena, in a solemn shrill voice.

The others had forgotten the child, in their interest in the nuns.

"Very likely they are," said Bessie, "so now let us go to dinner."

CHAPTER XVII.

THE CAMELLINA.

ONE day when Miss Lejeune was waiting for a car to bring her back to town after a bath, she glanced through an open doorway to a patio more than usually attractive. The entrance was dark, so that its opening made a great square of light and sunshine, and this is what she saw: — tall pillars supported the roof of the corridor which ran round the court. The side she could see was covered with the luxuriant growth of the Camellina winding round the pillars, creeping along the edge of the roof, covering it, climbing on to the flat roof of the house, and stretching up against the chimneys and toward the sky. Climbing roses were there too, but the Camellina overpowered them, its long wreaths of blossoms, a sort of solferino pink, hanging about over the green. The house with its corridors occupied only three sides of the square court. The one opposite the street entrance was bounded with a light iron railing, and beyond stretched the huerta, or orchard, a wild place containing tall shade-trees, fruit-trees and a tangle of roses, honeysuckle and sweet peas. The courtyard was laid with flat stones, and the floor of the corridor with red tiles running diagonally. Red pots for flowers were set along the railing, which was overgrown with roses, great white ones, others like Jacqueminots, Maréchal Niels, and such like greenhouse varieties.

While Miss Lejeune was looking at the whole with delight, and thinking how pretty it would be for a sketch, if she only could do it, a *muchacha* came out from a door in the side of the house with a baby in her arms. In her feeble Spanish Miss Lejeune apologized for being there, and expressed her admiration of the beautiful vine. Just then a young Mexican woman appeared, perhaps the mother of the child and the lady of the house. She was most hospitable, and begged Miss Lejeune to pass through the court and examine the garden. Unluckily at that moment was heard the rumble of the car, and the click of the mule's feet.

"*Mi caro!*" exclaimed Miss Lejeune, and turned reluctantly to go: she had time to express a great wish to return and even to attempt a sketch of the patio. It was most cordially granted, and she joyfully stepped into the car which passed directly by the door, calling back a friendly "*Hasta luego, mañana.*"

Of course a dozen things happened to prevent her going the next day and the next. A great mail arrived from the States, and there were letters to answer. Little Helena was not very well, having eaten too many of her favorite plums,— bright scarlet, slightly acid, chiefly stone in the middle, but very delicious, the little girl thought.

So it was the third morning afterwards that Miss Lejeune set forth again armed with all her sketching materials, and as she rode along in the car watched anxiously for her patio. She was not sure of finding it, for all was so like the *Arabian Nights*, it seemed quite possible that it would have disappeared entirely. A long row of blank walls, and close-shut iron-barred windows encouraged this feeling, but suddenly the sunlight flashed again from the bright opening. She stopped the car, alighted, and stood again in the doorway, a little frightened at her own boldness.

"Perhaps they have forgotten," she thought; "perhaps that family has moved away; perhaps the lady I saw was not the head of the family, perhaps,— there is a big dog!"

But none of these things were right, for as soon as she appeared, several muchachas swarmed out and welcomed her as an expected guest, asking what she required. She modestly demanded a chair.

They brought two, then a straw-matting to put under her feet on the stone floor. Then a round table for the materials, then more water to paint with. They were brown maidens neatly dressed in light-colored print gowns, their straight black hair braided in two long tails to the waist, their teeth very white, and their "*Sí, Señorita,*" accompanied always by a friendly smile.

From the side of the house she could not see,— for she was sitting in the passageway so that only one angle of the court was visible,— she heard an elderly woman's voice directing all these little attentions, and occasionally saw a tall, pleasant-looking lady in a gray dress moving about who did not come near. But soon the younger lady came and greeted her and watched the beginning of her work; then she went away, and from some room not far off, Miss Lejeune heard her playing brilliantly upon a fine piano. The house was but one story high, with rooms adjoining each other, all opening upon the corridor, none upon the street.

Miss Lejeune worked away for a couple of hours with more vigor than skill, her mind distracted by her desire to overflow with gratitude in her best Spanish to all these people. She heard the elderly lady giving directions to a servant, who, in consequence, brought out a tall ladder and climbed to the roof. He began to gather clusters of the pink blossom; the hidden voice kept saying, "Not enough, larger," until he laid hold of a long *ramo*, or branch of flowers as tall as himself.

This was presently brought to Miss Lejeune, to her great joy, for it was just what she was longing for, and then came a huge bunch of roses,— each worth seventy-five cents in Boston, at that season,— crimson, pink, yellow, white. Two gentlemen came from some unseen part of the house, who talked with her a little in English; one of them kissed the baby, said good-by, stopped the *caro* and went off to town.

The time flew. Miss Augusta dashed in washes, without stopping to judge the effect, smiled on the baby, nodded to the *muchachas*, who, as they stood looking on, more in amazement than pure admiration at her work, murmured every minute "muy hermosa," "muy bonita;" till, as she snatched a moment to look at her watch, she found she must take the next car, or be late to lunch. She went on working till the last moment, then hastily packed her things, corked her water-bottle, took the great bunch of roses and grasped the long wreath of camellina, scattering plentiful farewells among the group of friends.

The car came, she entered it with some difficulty, and almost filled it with her floral accompaniments. Luckily it was empty. A few doors farther on, two Mexican young women came into the car, who conversed together about her evidently, so she joined in their talk; they told her that their camellina was as beautiful as this camellina, that their home was on the opposite side of the Calzada, and that the señorita was welcome to come and see theirs any day. Finding these ladies knew where she had been much better than she did herself, she ventured to ask the name of the family who lived in the sunny house. They told her it was the *casa de recreo* of a branch of one of the leading families; that is their summer retreat.

As she hoped, when Miss Lejeune came out of the car in front of the hotel, all her family were looking from the windows. Bessie leaning on her balcony, Tom hanging over his, Helena and Jack in that belonging to Miss Lejeune's room.

"What's this!" they called out, "what have you got?" The two children rushed away from the balcony, and came down-stairs like lightning and out into the street to help her with her "plunder." Pedro smiled a wan smile in the doorway. The German landlord proffered the usual "Guten Morgen," his American wife looked at the flowers, and Bessie and Tom met her on the landing.

"Where have you been!" they exclaimed, for she had not told them the beginning of the adventure lest it might not turn out well in the end.

This little event gave them all a pleasant idea of the hospitality of the Morelians, and it was everywhere justified by the constant kindness they received there and elsewhere. The people in the streets and shops whom they came to know during their little stay, watched them with a sort of friendly interest rather than intrusive curiosity, and were always ready to do them a friendly turn.

"What has happened to the rest of the family in my absence?" asked Miss Lejeune, when she had recovered her breath and told her little tale. Bessie meanwhile had put the branch of camellina in water, sacrificing the wash-stand jug to that purpose.

"Helena and I have been at home," she replied, "as we thought she had best not go out in the heat, and Tom and Jack have been to market."

"I should think so," said Miss Lejeune, for looking around the room, she perceived it to be full of flowers and fruit. "You seem to have transferred the market to our premises."

"It was such fun, aunt Dut," said Jack; "you must go again when all the people are there."

"We have seen the Host go by," said Bessie; "I am sorry you missed that."

She had happened to be looking out, and called Helena in time to see what they had often heard described. A carriage, just like any ordinary hack, drove by with a lighted candle within, showing that the last ceremonies of the church were to be administered to some dying person. The horses were white, and the driver had his hat off. As the carriage was seen approaching, every person who chanced to be in the street kneeled, and with bowed head waited its passing. As it receded in the distance they turned toward it, until it disappeared round a corner. It was strange to watch its progress, and to see them all one after another bow before it. There was no other carriage in sight, but a good many people were upon the sidewalks, all kneeling with bent heads, as if for the moment turned to stone.

CHAPTER XVIII.

THE AZTECS.

NOW I will tell you about the Aztecs," said Bessie, "the ancestors of the Montezuma whom Cortés found in Mexico. "The Aztecs started from Aztlan, it is thought, at the same time with the Tepanecs and all those other people whose names you have forgotten. This Aztlan is a mysterious place, referred to as the source of the early Indians of Mexico, but no one can say where it was. Perhaps if the Spaniards had not burnt up the hieroglyphics and pictures they found, we could know more about it, and perhaps your father, Jack, will find a temple all covered with carvings which will tell the whole story."

"Will he?" said Jack, with big eyes.

"That is what he hopes to do," replied Bessie, "and you can help him, and he will be pleased to find that you know something about these old people.

"The situation of Aztlan is most obscure. It has been guessed to be in California, in Florida, and other places in America. Whenever explorers find traces of old civilization in North America, they wonder if these were left by the people who wandered away into Mexico; and if they were, why did they leave Aztlan, some first, others afterward, with such great differences between that when their descendants came together in Mexico, they had nothing in common, scarcely a trace of the same language, and generally fought like cats and dogs?

"The Azt-ecs took their name from Azt-lan, you see. The date of their leaving it is wholly uncertain, but perhaps they started in the middle of the seventh century; they stopped long years in one place after another, and built houses and temples, whose ruins may still be seen. About six hundred years after they came to the shores of Lake Tezcuco, where the city of Mexico is now."

"Not the same ones that started!" said Jack.

"No, not at all; but their great-great-great-grandsons."

"Anyhow, the Aztecs used up a long time on their way, and arrived at Chapultepec somewhere about 1200. They were in con-

RUINS FOUND IN YUCATAN.

stant difficulty in the beginning; conquered by their neighbors, they took refuge in the midst of marshes on almost inaccessible islands. They were also called Mexican from one of their gods named Mexitli, who wished them to be named after him, according to their priests.

"During their wanderings, they seem for the first time to have taken up the custom of sacrificing human beings upon the altars of their gods, and this made them unpopular among other tribes who had not the same practice."

"Finally they came upon an island where they found a *nopal* growing out of a stone, and upon the leaves of the nopal an eagle was sitting with a snake in his clutches,—rather a remarkable combination. The priests said that was the place their god Mexitli would like them to select for a city, where they should settle down and cease from wandering."

"What is a nopal?" asked Helena.

"You know," said Bessie, "it is that great cactus we see everywhere with leaves that look like mittens with fat fingers sticking out. Those fingers are the blossoms, and by and by every one of them will turn into a fruit, called a *tuna*, very cool and refreshing."

ANCIENT VASE FOUND IN MISSOURI.

So they began their city and called it Tenochtitlan which means "place of the stone and the nopal."

The Mexican flag has the stone and the nopal and the snake and the eagle all on it.

The Mexicans (or Aztecs) had a miserable life for a long time, at odds with all the people about them. They managed to strengthen their island with stones and earth, and they created floating islands in the neighborhood where they planted maize and other things. Thus they grew stronger; living by hunting and fishing, their population increased rapidly. Their alliance with the Tepanees, when they all overcame the Chichimees, was a great thing for the Mexicans, for from that time they became powerful, till, from the marshes where they first took refuge, their power spread all over the country. They made conquests everywhere, only through the superior strength of their arms, for no other nation sought their alliance. They oppressed the peoples they conquered, and used the prisoners they took in war as sacrifices upon their altars in honor of victory. In fact they made war to bring in victims to satisfy, as they imagined, the demands of their gods.

Mexico, their capital, grew to be a splendid city, filled with palaces and temples. It was a sort of Venice, connected with the main land by causeways, and protected by dikes, and as the water of the lake was salt, aqueducts were built from Chapultepec, to lead fresh water to the capital.

The Aztec princes lived in the greatest splendor, in spacious palaces, and wore lovely robes of feather-work, with gold ornaments and precious stones. The Mexicans knew the use of cotton which they cultivated,

MONTEZUMA.

and wove into cloth; in fact they became a most intelligent and enlightened people, gentle and refined in a great many ways; they knew a great deal about astronomy and the movements of the heavenly bodies, the division of time according to the sun's course; their picture-writings were wonderful. It seems strange that they have such a horrible religion, which made them shed human blood upon their altars, for many of their rites were simple and graceful, accompanied by decoration with flowers.

When a chief died the body was covered with a mantle richly embroidered, and precious stones. Little pieces of paper of different shapes were laid on the corpse, and as he gave each one to the dead, the priest said, "With this you will be able to cross the passage between the two mountains; this one is a pass across the great desert and the eight hills; this will enable you to avoid the great serpent, etc."

They used to kill a little red-haired dog to bury him with the corpse, with a leash about his neck. This dog was to guide his master over nine great torrents he would have to cross.

When the dead person was not rich or distinguished enough to be buried with such pomp and splendor, the relations and friends brought flowers, food and clothes to be buried with him. The idea always was to furnish the dead with materials for a life like that on this earth.

Thus the Mexicans grew to be the most powerful of all the nations of Anahuac, but they were not beloved, for all the others feared them, and dreaded to fall into their power, on account of being sacrificed as victims. So when Cortés came into the country, he learned that the other tribes would not be sorry to have the Aztecs brought low. At the beginning of the sixteenth century, Montezuma the Second was reigning,— for there had been another king of the same name about fifty years before. This second one was only twenty-three years old when he came to the throne. He was grave, tranquil, taciturn, inflexible in his judgments, disliking to be contradicted, severe and cruel in carrying out his will, and very superstitious. As soon as he began to reign he increased the state and splendor which surrounded the monarch,

THE AZTECS.

displayed great luxury on his person and in his palace, established forms and ceremonies with the object of elevating the king to a divinity in the eyes of his subjects; for all this it was necessary to increase the taxes until they became oppressively heavy.

About this time there were strange presages and warnings which greatly disturbed the superstitious king and his people, for they announced some dreadful cataclysm to come. Temples were burned, comets appeared, there were earthquakes and inundations and all sorts of things, and amongst it all, rumors of a superior race of men coming from the East, all white, with beards,— for the Aztecs did not have beards to speak of,— who were coming to subjugate all the nations of the land. These rumors preceded the arrival of Cortés, so that when Montezuma heard about his really being near, and about his strange animals with men's heads beside their own, he was frightened; and no wonder. At first he sent ambassadors to the Spaniard, with splendid presents, politely saying that he could not allow him on any account to come to his capital.

But Cortés did not mind that in the least; he went right on, and, after conquering the Tlaxcallans, made peace with them, and increased his army with these new allies, and so on, till he finally presented himself in Mexico on the eighth of November, 1519.

He was received by Montezuma by great pomp and circumstance, although the poor king was so frightened that it was only after much hesitation that he could bring his mind to receive the strangers.

The Spaniards took their way from Tlaxcala, between the two volcanoes Popocatepetl and Ixtaccihuatl, by Amaquemecan, now Amecameca, and so along the lakes Chalco and Xochicalco.

"Is that the way we came?" asked Jack.

"No," said Bessie. "The Vera Cruz road comes round the northern side of Lake Tezcuco, as poor old Cortés had to come out, as I will tell you later."

"When Bessie and I went down to Orizaba to meet you," said Tom, "we could see glimpses of that side of the lake."

"We did not see much that evening we arrived," said Miss Lejeune; "what a dreary ride that was. When we are in Mexico again we must go over that ground."

"Yes," said Bessie, "and go down to Amecameca, which is so near the volcanoes that there is a lovely view of them, they say, like that of the Alps at Chamouni."

"Is it easy to go there?" asked Miss Lejeune.

"O yes! there is a railroad."

"I cannot help laughing," she said, "at the bare idea of railroads in connection with the Spaniards. It would have been an immense convenience to Cortés if he could have stepped into a special train with all his troops, just to run up to the city."

"Yet the Spaniards flattered themselves," said Bessie, "that they were introducing all the modern improvements,— gunpowder and fire-arms,"—

"And horses," said Jack.

"Yes, and a new religion," added Miss Lejeune.

"And the habit of taking what did not belong to them," remarked Tom.

"We must remember," said Bessie, "that it was the ruling principle of that time that heathens were of no consequence. Just as Ferdinand and Isabella thought they were doing a great service to the true Faith, and making themselves glorious, by the conquest of Granada, Cortés considered his course with the Mexicans one strong proof of his devotion to the advance of the Cross. I believe he was very much in earnest in this, and he thought he was in the performance of the highest duty, if he converted the Indians when he could, and killed them when he could not."

CHAPTER XIX.

HELENA'S ADVENTURE.

DO you think we had better buy our serapes here," asked Miss Lejeune, "or wait till we go back to Mexico?"

"Jack and I saw some beauties in the *portales* behind the Cathedral," said Tom.

"Let us go there to-morrow morning, then," said Miss Lejeune; "and suppose we start early and go to see the market, for I have never been thoroughly through it."

"Very well," said Tom, "to-morrow will be a good day for the market;" and so it was agreed.

Directly after coffee they all sallied forth, and after a very short walk found themselves in the market-place, one of the open squares of the town, nearly all covered over with awnings, underneath which were booths with a passageway between. Within each booth an Indian woman presided over her wares, keeping neatly arranged upon low wooden tables set in a hollow square, little pyramids of bright plums, dark-skinned alborotes, oranges, limes, bananas, and other strange fruits. As soon as the party appeared, it was surrounded by a swarm of bright-faced *muchachos*, carrying empty baskets. Tom chose one, driving off the others, and the selected boy, smiling from ear to ear, followed them close, with his basket upon his shoulder. They went from stall to stall, attracted by some strange new fruit, or the superior lusciousness of some especial pile.

"We must try everything," said Miss Lejeune; "have we had any of these?" pointing to a black mass that looked like a decayed india-rubber ball.

"They are terrible," said Bessie, "but perhaps you had better have some. Ah! here are mangoes!"

It was early for mangoes, and the wise in such matters assured them that the ones then to be had were not fair specimens of the fruit; but Bessie had learned already to like them.

"To be sure," she said, "they smell like sponge-blacking, and taste like turpentine, but they are not so sickishly sweet as these other things."

Most of the unknown fruits in the market were products of the *tierra caliente*, and therefore of a tropical nature, so given over to sweetness that they lack, to Northern palates at least, the individual flavor of a good peach, pear or apple. The mango, however, is not too sweet, and when fully ripe, is juicy and delicious. It has a huge stone in the middle. A thing called a mango fork, with one tine, is used to stick well into the stone at the stem end, thus serving as a handle, while the fruit, a little like a flat pear, is peeled from end to end. The rind is thick and yellow. It leaves the flesh around the stone, looking like winter squash, juicy and luscious. It must be eaten like corn from the cob; the stone is left covered with the shreds just as a cling-stone peach is.

"There is a feverish joy about eating a mango. One is hoping always it will be better than the last, and generally thinking it is not so good."

This was Miss Lejeune's verdict one day at a restaurant table.

"Ah, Madame," said a man who understood English, but talked French, "you should eat them in Cordova, in the true season; they would then allay your fever."

In the market, each bought for a trifle what he liked, and threw it into the basket upon the boy's back, which began to bend beneath the load of good things. After passing through the fruit-region of the market, they came to one of the sidewalks of the square, where pots and pans of native make were displayed upon the ground. These were perfectly fascinating to our people, just as the pottery of Spain had been. They never could pass a collection without stopping to look at it, and could seldom resist buying a few jugs or dishes, while sighing over the hopelessness of packing them to reach home safe. Many a jug cost only a *tlaco*, a small sum of money, worth a cent and a half. There are cents, and cents cut in two, actually, to represent this sum, the next coin being a *cuartillo*, worth three cents; but the half-cents are scarce, and the dark vendors often had no change. There was much running about, and searching in pockets for small coins, which often ended in the purchase of a saucer or a pottery bird, price a cent and a half, to make up the sum.

The Aztecs moulded pottery on a large scale; and some interesting specimens of their work are preserved. The modern Mexicans show much taste and skill in its manufacture, both in simple grace of form, and in color. There is a great difference in the excellence and beauty of the pottery of different towns. That of Guadalajara is the best. It is glazed, and variegated in color, and some of the many designs into which it is moulded are most artistic. Guadalajara ware may sometimes be found in other markets. The Horners searched for it in Morelia, for they had seen a lovely vase of this ware which was bought in Morelia, but in vain. There was none to be found. The Morelia ware was pretty, however; little brown jugs of the simplest form, sometimes tinted with green, were irresistible. Their table at the hotel was covered with a fleet of these little jugs, slightly differing from each other in size, form, color, and expression. They were most useful to hold the flowers, equally irresistible, to be bought in the market.

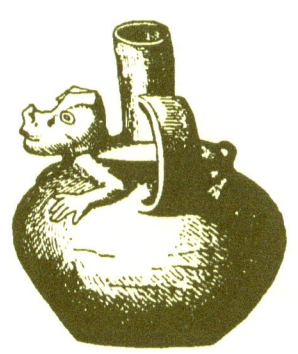

ANCIENT AZTEC VASE.

They turned reluctantly from the pottery, followed by their boy, whose basket contained now on top of the fruit a layer of jugs, two pottery whistles in the shape of birds, a rude bull of the same material, and two flat dishes which Miss Lejeune said she must have, although Tom assured her there were six at home just like them.

The place was swarming now with Morelians, some there to buy, some to sell. The next sidewalk they came to was in front of a church, and the traffic stretched back under its portal. Here native women, over charcoal, were cooking fearful messes which others bought and ate with relish. Milk, or pulque, was served to these customers in little jugs like those for sale round the corner. Meat, fish and fowls, — which passed alive, hanging by the neck, from hand to hand, — were bought and sold. A simple advertisement of these latter was a proud rooster tied by the leg, and parading about at the utmost length of his tether. Next came the old junk collections, spread flat upon the ground. These possessed a great attraction for Tom, who was always expecting to pick up some treasure among them, for a *tlaco*. Old locks, old keys, the wrong half of a jack-knife, a single scissor, glass bottles, torn books which might contain the lost history of the early migrations, — all sorts of things. There was a pair of green spectacles with goggle eyes and gold bows which Bessie longed to buy, but Miss Lejeune urged her not to, lest they might have the small-pox. It seemed not likely, but they did not discuss the matter, wandering idly on to the flower-stalls in the middle of the square.

Here were heaps of sweet-peas, huge bunches of gaudy poppies, every possible shade of red, from flaming orange to deep-crimson, big masses of white roses, pink roses, red roses, all so cheap, — and the women clamoring for notice, each holding up a tempting show.

"Helena, here are your favorite pansies," said Miss Lejeune, then added, — "where is Helena! Bessie, is she with you?"

As usual, they are surrounded by natives, watching their bargains, and thus were somewhat separated.

"No!" cried Bessie, threading her way back to Miss Augusta; "where are Tom and Jack? she must be with them."

But she was not with them. The little girl was not to be seen. With dismay they looked each other in the face, and then set about hurrying from one stall to another, retracing their steps as well as they could, and looking eagerly at the brown faces of the native children for their little pale European. It would have been easy to distinguish her if she had been there, with her light curls, straw hat and dark blue cambric dress, among the shock-headed brown Indians in picturesque, but slovenly attire.

As soon as the basket-boy grasped the situation, he offered to search for her.

"Do you know her?" asked Tom impatiently, in Spanish.

"O yes," the boy replied, "he had often seen the *Niña* on the balcony."

"Well, give your basket to this other boy, and you go in search for her. Aunt Dut, you and Bessie had best go home with the boy and the basket, and I will stay and look. Jack, you go with the ladies."

Jack would fain have stayed, but the idea of being escort to the ladies pleased him, so they started off sorrowfully toward the hotel.

"Perhaps she will be there!" he suggested, and this, though unlikely, made them hasten their steps. She was not at the hotel, no one had seen her.

"Are you sure, Pedro, you have not seen the Señorita Helena?" asked Bessie, sternly.

The sad Pedro mournfully shook his head, and raised his hands to show that they were empty of all knowledge of the Señorita.

"I could shake him," said Bessie, as they went up stairs. "He need not look so stupid, if he did not know anything about her!"

There was nothing to do but to go and lean on the balcony, imagining all sorts of dreadful things, hoping the best. Half an hour passed, an hour, the street seemed unusually empty, silent, deserted. Bessie saw the landlord below, leaning against the door, and ran down to consult him in German. He good-naturedly started for the market, to help in the search, where he soon came upon Tom, trying to rouse the people there to some interest. They were all more or less like Pedro; they shrugged their shoulders, opened their hands, and went on about their own business.

Miss Lejeune had left the balcony, and was trying to count out the wash. Suddenly Bessie called out, "Come here! I do believe —"

Far in the distance, from the direction just opposite the market, they saw a *muchacho* leading a little girl. It must be Helena! They were coming slowly, for the child walked as if she were tired. Some instinct had taken the boy through a street leading to the *portales*.

"When I found I was lost," said Helena, "I remembered you meant to buy *serapes*, and all of a sudden I saw the house with the camellinas, and I thought that street would lead to the *portales*, because I was there with Tom when he went to the post-office."

"But how did you get there at all?" asked Bessie.

"I dropped my bird, and his tail broke off," said Helena, "and I cried; so the woman gave me a whole one, and so I said 'gracias,' and ran after you, but I never could see you any more!" The recollection made her unhappy again, but they soothed her.

The *muchacho*, standing by, told how he had inquired of the bird-sellers, and they had pointed out the direction she had taken. He hurried along, and overtook her walking bravely on the way to the portales, looking neither to right nor left.

"I was almost afraid to go with him," said Helena, "for they all look alike, but he pointed this way and said 'Jack,— hermano!' and besides, I was so glad to go with somebody."

The adventure had been brief, but uncomfortable, and they were all glad it was over. The *muchacho* ran back to the market, found Tom, and sent him home happy. The boy was well-fed, and greatly petted by them all ever afterward.

CHAPTER XX.

A SUDDEN DEPARTURE.

THE best places for *serapes* is San Miguel, but the Horners were not going there, although they would have liked to, and it was not far out of their way. It is a station on the National railway, at present the northern terminus of that line, which branches at Acambaro toward Morelia on the west. It is a picturesque town, and interesting on account of its baths, built of stone, with an arcaded front, facing a terrace with stone seats, from which there is a lovely view of the town sloping down a hillside to fields and meadows. The water of these baths is said to leave a most refreshing effect upon the skin. In the neighborhood of the town are rural lanes and pretty gardens.

This part of Mexico is associated with the history of Mexican liberty, for not far from San Miguel is Dolores de Hidalgo, where, near midnight, on September 15, 1810, the famous *grito de independencia* was raised. The revolution began the next day. It was a struggle of eleven years, of which the ultimate result was the independence of the Mexican nation. The confusion in Spain caused by the weakness of Charles the Fourth, and the bad government of his favorite Godoy, had given Napoleon Bonaparte an opportunity to lay his grasp upon that country. By the beginning of 1808, he had made himself master of the most important cities of the Peninsula. Charles was compelled to abdicate, and Ferdinand the Seventh, his son and lawful heir, made to renounce the crown of Spain in favor of Joseph Bonaparte. On the second of May, the people of Madrid rose against the French, and this was the signal for a general insurrection against the invaders. Different *juntas* were formed, under a central one, who governed in the name of Ferdinand the Seventh. The viceroys of New Spain,— Mexico,— obeyed the mandates of this junta, without ever recognizing Joseph Bonaparte as their king. All this disturbance in the old country diminished the prestige of Spanish authority in the new, and prepared all minds for insurrection. In the end of 1809 a conspiracy was discovered in Valladolid (now Morelia) and its leaders were thrown into prison. Another was instantly formed in

QUERETARO.

Querétaro, and of the new movement the soul and chief was Don Miguel Hidalgo. He was educated as a priest, was a man of talent, of wide and varied information, and of opinions advanced for the time in which he lived. He cultivated the vine and mulberry in Dolores, and was an industrious and loyal citizen, although suspected by the ruling parties on account of his liberal opinions. Such was the man who, when the time came, devoted his life to the independence of his country, and to whom the leading place was given among the first conspirators.

At dawn on the sixteenth of September, at mass in Dolores, Hidalgo caused independence to be proclaimed, by a little body of eighty men, which soon increased to three hundred, who marched out towards San Miguel. Hidalgo gave his little army, for a banner, a picture of the Virgin of Guadalupe, belonging to the church of a little village on the way. The battle-cry was, "Long live Religion, and down with bad government!" A leading motive with Hidalgo in the insurrection was a fear that religion would suffer if Napoleon should rule in Mexico as well as in Spain, and this is said to be the reason why the priests, as they did, took an active part in the struggle. But later, the Church proved an obstacle in the way of liberty, and this was not really attained in Mexico until the Church was forever separated from the State in

THE MORNING MARCH.

the great civil war which brought about the reform constitution of 1857.

The first great step in the revolution was the taking of Guanajuato, a large and rich city. Hidalgo then took up his march to Mexico over a route not unlike that of the National Railway, passing however through Morelia or Valladolid, as it then was. His army grew at every step, and numbered a hundred thousand men as he approached the capital. The Spaniards, panic-stricken after a bloody combat on the thirtieth of October, might, it would seem, have been easily overcome, but Hidalgo remained in camp, and then he for some strange reason, retreated towards Querétaro. He was overtaken, and lost all his advantages. His fortunes from that time declined, and this first chapter of Mexican Independence, but by no means the last, ended on July 30, 1811, with the shooting of Hidalgo, and three others who were leaders with him.

THE VIRGIN OF GUADALUPE.

"I wish we could go to San Miguel," said Miss Lejeune.

"Why do we not?" asked Tom, who was lolling back in the great bamboo balançoire, which always looked as if it must go over backwards the very next minute. Miss Lejeune winced as she looked up at him, for close behind him in the pitcher was the tall camellina, supported against the side of the window.

"If you should go over, Tom,—" she said, looking past him at the flowers.

"Your *ramo* would be spoiled, the water spilt, and the jug smashed," said Tom, finishing the sentence, and then he added, "the trifling circumstance of my breaking my neck would be merely thrown in." He got up and went out upon the balcony, saying as he went, "Why do we not go to San Miguel?"

"Then we need not buy the scrapes here," suggested Bessie.

"And we could go back on the Mexican Central to Mexico," said Tom.

"The thing is whether we have time," said Miss Lejeune; "Mr. Johnstone may be ready to take the children any day now."

"It is rather provoking of the Johnstones not to write," grumbled Tom.

"Mrs. Johnstone writes the children every day," said Miss Lejeune, with half a laugh.

"Yes," said Tom, "but she never says anything. Here come the children with the mail," he continued, and leaning over the balcony, called out, "Halloo, Jack! any letters?"

"No end!" was the answer, and Jack held up a big package of them. The *muchacho*, hero of Helena's rescue, who had been with them to the post-office, smiled from ear to ear. They all disappeared under the doorway, but the two children were soon in the room.

"Here is one from mama; will you read me mama's, Bessie?" said Helena, while Jack distributed the others. Bessie looked longingly at her own pile from home which lay in her lap, but she patiently deciphered for the little girl the graceful, but somewhat illegible note from her mother.

"My dear darlings," it said, "for you must both of you accept this, although it is only addressed to Helena. I love you very much and long every morning and every evening to see you. Papa is very busy, and I am very tired with seeing how much he has to do, but sometimes he has time to take me a lovely drive in the beautiful paseos, where we see the lofty volcanoes. You must be very, very good children and not trouble our dear kind friends, and Helena must try not to lose her pocket handkerchiefs, for there will be no one in Yucatan to hem new ones but poor mama " —

"Why!" exclaimed Miss Augusta over the top of her letters just as Bessie had reached this point. Tom was lifting his eyebrows in an expressive manner for Bessie's benefit, implying that as usual Mrs. Johnstone's letter contained little in the way of information.

"This is a telegram!" Miss Lejeune went on. "How stupid! they sent it to the post-office." From Mr. Johnstone:—

Obliged to take next steamer. Send children at once.

The Horners and Miss Augusta looked blankly at each other, and Jack began to weep audibly.

"I do not want to go away!" he cried.

"Jack," said Tom sternly, "what is the matter with you? Be a man, sir!"

Jack was immediately silent, and slipped from the room.

"Tom, you ought to go after him," pleaded Bessie.

"No, no," said Tom, who was deeply displeased, "let us discover the meaning of these orders at once. Let us see; how much are our wages for fetching and carrying the Johnstones?"

"Don't be absurd, Tom," said Miss Lejeune, "or at least postpone your wrath. The thing is now to see what we are to do. We should have received the telegram yesterday."

"His steamer," said Bessie, "leaves Thursday. They must go down to Vera Cruz at least Tuesday, and probably prefer to start Monday. To-day is Saturday. If we go through to-morrow, we shall get there in time."

Tom walked up and down the room in a rage. The two ladies were silent.

"Let us send the children by themselves," he said. "They will go fast enough."

"Put them in a bag, properly labelled," suggested Miss Lejeune lightly, with the view of allaying his wrath.

"We might send Pedro with them," said Bessie.

Helena began to pucker up her face.

"Now, do not you begin, pray," said Bessie, and then breaking into laughter, she swept her off into Miss Lejeune's room, putting her head back through the door of communication to say, "You two settle it, and Helena and I will get Jack, and go and see about the wash."

Bessie knew well that it would end in a sudden departure at daylight the next morning. She relied on Miss Augusta to bring Tom round, and went at once herself to take practical measures for breaking camp.

CHAPTER XXI.

LAKE CUITZAO.

IN the early morning, before light, next day, Pedro was knocking at the doors of the travellers. All the heavy baggage had been packed hurriedly the day before and carried off to the station on the sturdy backs of cargadores, and now, by the dim gleam of candles that cast but a feeble glow over the high bare rooms, last things were thrust into yawning mouths of handbags, straps were fastened, umbrellas gathered together.

Helena and Jack were ready and standing in the window to watch for the car, more than half an hour before there was the faintest chance of its appearing. Pedro also had been so impressed with the importance of securing the *caro*, that he had put the street-sweeper upon the watch.

Helena and Jack could see this dusky individual languidly brushing dust down the paved street toward the gutter that trickled through the middle of it. Lanterns flitted to and fro, and in the east was a pale gold streak of dawn. A man came by with sherbet to sell, at that unearthly hour, in a row of tumblers upon a board which he carried on his head.

When all was ready, Miss Lejeune and Bessie went below; Pedro brought them a couple of low chairs such as are very common in Mexico, not more than half a foot high, with broad seats and straight backs. Bessie had grown so fond of the one in her room that she wished to carry it back to the States with her, but it would have proved a troublesome piece of baggage.

Just before daylight is a dreary time of day to be up and

dressed and waiting for a street-car, with an empty stomach. The children were nibbling sweet cakes and skipping backward and forward from the street to the court. Tom had not yet appeared. The street was absolutely empty and quiet, for all Morelia was still asleep.

"I wish mamma could see us now," said Bessie, "how she would congratulate herself to be safe in bed."

"It is not bad to be up so early," said Miss Augusta, to make the best of it, "but I wish I had my coffee. See how the light is creeping along the street!"

"How strange it all is!" said Bessie. "I wonder if we shall ever be here again?"

"I hope so," said Miss Lejeune; "it is so easy to come, when you once are started. It is a pity we could not do Patzcuaro this time. O yes! I feel sure we shall come again."

Just then Tom came down and joined them, with a young American gentleman to whom they had been introduced only the night before.

"Mr. Pastor is going as far as Acambaro with us," said Tom, as that gentleman shook hands with the ladies.

"How pleasant!" said Miss Lejeune cordially; "that will make us a *partie carrée*, and you can explain everything to us."

"I ought to be able to," he replied, "as I go over the road several times a week."

Mr. Pastor occupied an important post on the National Railway, which required him at present to make his headquarters in Morelia, and to be frequently going back and forth over the line.

"I am very sorry," he said, "to have done nothing to make you enjoy Morelia. I have been detained all this time in Mexico, and only just heard from Mr. Purdy that you were here. I hastened back as quickly as I could, hoping you could stay sometime longer."

"So we should," began Tom, "if it had not been —"

"For unforeseen circumstances," finished Bessie, glancing at the children in a warning manner. "Hark, methinks I hear our car!"

A low dull rumbling was to be heard, and far off at the end of the street bounded by the arches of the aqueduct, the car might be dimly discerned, the only moving object visible. It was still long before it reached them. Pedro arrested it with violent gestures, which must have exhausted him for the day, unused as he was to vigorous exercise. They filed across the street and stepped into the car, waving farewells to Pedro and wishing silent ones to the silent town which they had grown to love very much. The car jogged on; the party relapsed into corners, still sleepy, and dull from lack of food.

It was long before the station was reached, for the car stopped to wait for passengers who apparently had not left their beds until roused by the tooting of the horn. But there was plenty of time, and at the station they all went into a little hut where delicious coffee was served by an aged niña whose long braids were growing gray. In Mexico all women are *niñas* whatever age they may be, although the word means "little girl." It is a remnant of the politeness of the old Castilian language, which overlooks the march of time in the fair sex.

Once more the party were seated in the crimson-covered seats of the narrow-gauge car, their belongings hung up above them, or tucked under the seats. It was full daylight now and promised a bright, clear day for Lake Cuitzao. They had the car all to themselves, and the children placed themselves each at a window on the left side, which would be the side of the lake. The others were all together, and Mr. Pastor made the way pleasant by pointing out objects of interest as they passed. Miss Lejeune, after her coffee, was lively and full of questions, which he answered with the greatest readiness.

"Do tell us about Patzcuaro," she said; "you have been there, of course."

"O yes, several times," he replied. "It is a great pity you did not go."

"It is a rough journey, is it not?"

"Well, yes, if you are not used to diligence; but it pays for all the fatigue. It is a hard day's ride, and the road is horrible, but the view of Patzcuaro, as you approach, with its beautiful lake studded with islands, is very fine."

Patzcuaro is said to be unlike any other Mexican city. It is a pretty little town, with sloping roofs on the shore of its lake in front of a little Indian village, built on a small island in the middle of the lake. On the opposite shore is Tzinzunzan, the capital of the ancient kingdom of Michoacan, where the king lived who was friendly to Cortés. It is said that his majesty came as far as Patzcuaro to meet his Spanish ally when he entered this territory.

"When you come another year," said Mr. Pastor, "the railway will be finished, I hope, as far as Patzcuaro, and it will be easy to go then. You will be sure to enjoy going out on the lake. And then you must go on to Uruápan."

"What, still farther!" said Miss Lejeune.

"Oh! you have done nothing unless you go to Uruápan," he said, smiling; "the road is most wild and picturesque, Salvator-like, and the village a tranquil little spot, buried in fruit trees, and coffee plantations."

Mr. Pastor told them about his expedition to Manzanillo, on the western coast of Mexico, when he belonged to a party of surveyors for the route of the national railway which is some day to connect the Rio Grande with the Pacific.

"That is," said he, smiling, "if the Mexican Government does not withhold the subsidy it gives us now."

"Is that possible?" asked Tom.

"It is more than likely, I am afraid," replied Mr. Pastor, and he went on to explain to Tom the financial position of the railways; but Miss Lejeune interrupted them to look at Lake Cuitzao, which they were now approaching, and as they rode close along its banks, they were fully occupied in exclamations of delight at its lovely shores, the lines of hills which bound it, and its bright sparkling waters. The children saw birds enough to satisfy them fully. White cranes standing on one leg, ducks swimming and diving, and flocks of small birds sweeping over the lake and settling in black swarms. Mr. Pastor told them there was plenty of shooting in the season. The lake is very shallow, although eighteen miles long.

BIRDS ON THE LAKE.

He told the children about Mr. Purdy's car, which has "sleepers," and a kitchen attached, so that he can stop and live on a siding of the railroad wherever and whenever he likes. And Mr. Pastor once came with a little party in this car to Lake Cuitzao. The two ladies lived in the car by the side of the lake while the gentlemen went off shooting. They were gone all day, and came back at night to a jolly little dinner deliciously cooked, slept like tops and went off again in the morning. One of the gentlemen stayed with the ladies, that they need not be afraid, and they sketched and read aloud, and gathered flowers along the shore of the lake.

"I hope the ladies were nice," said Tom.

"They were perfectly charming," said Mr. Pastor, with something like a sigh, after which he was silent for some time. Miss Augusta instantly formed a romance of the most intense nature, in connection with this part of Mr. Pastor's discourse. She told Bessie afterwards that she was sure there was a young lady in the case, and a deep and hopeless attachment. So she was disappointed later when she learned that one of the ladies of this camping-party, described so eloquently by Mr. Pastor, was married, and absolutely devoted to her husband, one of the most agreeable of men, and the other lady was a confirmed spinster, over fifty.

Mr. Pastor was a decided success. He jumped out at way stations and brought back strange things to eat which they had not dared to try before; *tomalies*, made of indian meal done up in a corn-husk, with a little bit of meat hidden within; they are very hot with *chili*, a kind of pepper much used in Mexico, and are also hot from the charcoal fire on which they have just been cooked. They can be held in the hand much like a banana and eaten in the same way. Bessie thought them excellent; but Miss Augusta was doubtful about the origin of the meat.

"It might be donkey, you know," she said.

"No matter," said Bessie, "as it is good. Oh! do give me another."

In this way the day passed rapidly, and they found themselves at the end of it without fatigue, although they had now done the whole distance in one day which had before been broken by a night at Toluca. The peak of Toluca was distinctly visible all the afternoon.

It was dark when they entered the city. Jules, as before, met them, and it was with a distinct feeling of home that they drove once more back to the hospital Café Anglais.

CHAPTER XXII.

TWO PATRIOTS.

BESSIE found time during the journey to go on with her bits of historical information for the benefit of the children. Before they left Morelia for good she wished them to know about the events which led to its change of name from Valladolid, which the Viceroy Mendoza had given it, to its present one.

The execution of Hidalgo, and his three friends, Allende, Aldama, and Jimenez, put an end to the first period of the war of Independence. Their heads were taken to Guanajuato, and hung up at the four corners of the Alhóndiga, or public granary, where they remained till 1821. The other leaders of the movement went about spreading ideas of independence.

In 1891 José Maria Morelos y Pavon began to distinguish himself. He was born in Valladolid, in 1765. His parents of humble origin, and poor, made a muleteer of him, and in this occupation he remained until he was thirty years old. Feeling inclined to study he entered the old college of San Nicolás in his native town, where the rector at that time was the patriot Hidalgo. Morelos made rapid progress in his studies, was ordained, and obtained one after another several curacies. After the proclamation at Dolores, he offered his services to the independents, and became the chief of a little band which grew to be a large army, moving from place to place to annoy the royalist forces; and gaining importance from day to day. He established the first Mexican Congress, which made its declaration of independence, and decreed the liberty of the slaves. After many vicissitudes, Morelos, taken prisoner at last, was conducted to Mexico, and shot on the twenty-second of December, 1815. He is regarded as a great hero in Mexico, and his native town glories in his memory. In 1828, when the Liberal Government, which owed its existence to these early patriots, was firmly established, the name of Morelia was given to the town "to honor the memory of its worthy son."

The house in which Morelos lived, in Morelia, contains his portrait, and a piece of cloth which served as a bandage for his eyes when he was shot, with some lines in Spanish beneath describing it as the venerated relic of a martyr. In front of the house is a commemoration tablet, saying:

> *Illustrious Morelos! Immortal Hero!*
> IN THIS HOUSE, ONCE HONORED BY YOUR PRESENCE,
> YOU ARE GRATEFULLY REMEMBERED
> BY THE PEOPLE OF MORELIA.

"Do tell me, Miss Horner," said Mr. Pastor, "did you go to see this house? How delightfully you have done the lions of the town."

"To tell you the truth, Mr. Pastor," Bessie replied, "I did not go near the house, to my knowledge, but I read all about it in a book."

"I do not exactly see," said Jack, "whom the liberals were fighting against. Why did not all the people in Mexico think the same way?"

"Because some of them were loyal to Ferdinand the Seventh, the rightful King of Spain. The viceroys did not suddenly cease to exist, you know, when Napoleon invaded Spain, and all the machinery of government in Mexico kept on going. The viceroy who happened to be ruling in Mexico when the news of the French invasion came was Don José Iturigaray. He tried to form a provisional government partly composed of natives; but the Spaniards in the capital who did not choose to have Mexicans meddle with public affairs, seized him and sent him to Spain as a prisoner Then the conspiracy of Hidalgo broke out, of which the intention was to drive the Spaniards from Mexico, don't you see?"

"I don't exactly see why the Mexicans were not Spaniards," said Jack; "they talked Spanish."

"It was not so very different," said Bessie, who liked to hear Jack speak out his difficulties, so that she could clear them up, "from the Yankees driving out the British at the time of the Revolution. They spoke English, you know."

"Oh, yes," said Jack, lighting up.

"It was different from the War of Independence of the United States in many ways," continued Bessie, "but like in some respects. The Mexican patriots, as Hildalgo, Morelos and the rest are called, were determined that Mexicans should be freed from Spanish rule, and have their own independent government.

"It was a long time before this came to pass. After the death of Morelos the patriots kept on fighting, but the regular troops were the most powerful, and the 'rebels' were gradually driven from the field, killed, imprisoned or forced to hide in the mountains where they lurked about like wild beasts.

"Royal authority now seemed to be fully reinstated in Mexico. The French were turned out of Spain, and the ignoble king, Ferdinand, had come back to the throne; but in the beginning of 1820, there was a revolution. The King was compelled to adopt a liberal constitution, and this again aroused the popular demand for a liberal government in Mexico. There was an officer in the army, a native Mexican, who during the civil war had hitherto distinguished himself on the royalist side, named Don Augustin Iturbide; he now threw off his allegiance, and began the revolution again, by proclaiming Mexico independent. This was on the twenty-fourth of February, 1821.

"Iturbide proposed a plan of a constitutional monarchy for his country by which the crown should be offered to Ferdinand. This revolt was highly successful, and very popular. In the course of a short time the whole country recognized the authority of Iturbide, except the capital, where most of the Spaniards were, and he finally obtained possession of that.

"Iturbide was born in Valladolid, and so was a native Mexican; his father came from Pampeluna in Spain. His life is a strange picture of contrasts. At first he was a bitter enemy to the insurrection. It was he who with his army prevented Morelos from taking Valladolid, on the second of December, 1813, and his resistance to those he called rebels was a constant check to their cause. Afterwards he espoused that very cause, and rose rapidly to the highest position. On the twenty-seventh of September, 1821, he made his triumphal entrance into the capital with sixteen thousand men. The citizens received the independent army with enthusiasm, and celebrated with demonstrations of great joy the end of Spanish domination in Mexico, which had endured for three hundred years, and the beginning of free government won in heroic struggle opened by Hidalgo on the sixteenth of September, 1810.

"In a wonderfully short time the popularity of Iturbide grew so, that he was elected to be emperor of Mexico, under the title of Augustin the First: this happened on the eighteenth of May, 1822. But his glory was brief. People who preferred to be republicans resisted him with an army; he was soon shut up in the city of Mexico. He was forced to abdicate March 20, 1823, and left the country with his family, on board an English vessel which took them to Leghorn. Before his departure he issued a manifesto to the Mexican people, expressing the desire that they should be happy under the new order of things. Thus ended, one year after his proclamation, the brief monarchy of the Emperor, Iturbide."

"Was that the end of him?" asked Jack.

"No," said Bessie, "he came back in disguise to Mexico, although he had agreed to live abroad forever; it was found out that he had left Italy, and as soon as he landed he was recognized, seized for a public enemy, and condemned to be shot as a traitor.

He was executed on the nineteenth of July, 1824, only a few days after landing in the country.

"But now, Jack, you had better run about a little, for you must be stiff with sitting still, and I am hoarse with talking."

"Come along with me," said Tom, "and we will sit at the end platform and see the country."

Jack stretched himself, and slipped from his seat not unwillingly, and went to the back of the car where the track rolled out like a long ribbon behind the train as it moved swiftly along. Sometimes they wound about great curves backward and forward to cross a barren valley. They could see where they were going by the telegraph poles along the line, and sometimes, looking back across the plain, they saw a church, or railroad station quite near, in appearance, which they had passed long before, having made a great circuit to avoid impassible places.

"What an interesting career," said Miss Lejeune, after the children had left them. "Iturbide is just like the hero of a novel. He must have been a fascinating man to be so popular."

He was brave, active, handsome, and fond of display, but he lacked force of character, and his indecision at critical moments ruined him. There was no deep principle underlying his course; probably it was personal ambition which led him to desert the royal cause, rather than any patriotic love of freedom. No wonder he was blinded by vanity when he was proclaimed emperor, when his horses were taken from his carriage and he was drawn along the streets by the populace, amid shouts of triumph. It did not occur to him that he could be conspired against as he had conspired.

He made many warm personal friends who never failed in their allegiance to him; but this personal popularity was not enough to influence a whole nation.

The house where he was born, in Morelia, has an inscription upon it, giving the date of his birth, with the title,—*Libertador de Mexico.*

CHAPTER XXIII.

MEXICO AGAIN.

THE Horners and Miss Lejeune were established again in the city of Mexico, at their comfortable quarters, the Café Anglais, where they now felt themselves entirely at home. The Johnstones were gone, fairly off towards Vera Cruz, on their way back to Yucatan. The children parted from their kind friends with reluctance, and indeed they might, for Tom and Bessie had great patience with children, in fact, a kind of passion for talking to them and looking after them. Miss Lejeune disliked responsibility, but if that was on the shoulders of some one else, she enjoyed having children round, and, in fitful fashion, devoted herself to them when she felt like it.

Jack and Helena, rejoining their parents, were now likely to be left more to their own resources, for Mrs. Johnstone was not strong enough to be so entertaining as the brisk young Horners, and Mr. Johnstone, although a most genial and agreeable man, was not the kind to take much notice of little people.

"So here we are by ourselves," said Miss Augusta, the morning of the Johnstones' departure, "and we can do just what we please all day long."

"Now," said Bessie, "we can really devote ourselves to the sights of the city of Mexico; for, to tell the truth, we know nothing about them. I have noticed the Cathedral in a vague sort of way, in passing, and all the churches and squares, but I have not given my mind to them in the least."

"Nor I," said Miss Augusta; "the only building I am acquainted with, is that house all made of Moorish tiles, which we pass whenever we go anywhere. Have we a map?"

"Why do you ask?" said Bessie with a laugh. "Of course, Tom bought one the first time he went out." She found it, and said, "You see, aunt Dut, that Mexico is laid out in straight streets at right angles with each other, for the most part; this is very simple. The only confusing thing is the naming of the streets, which changes all the time; that is, the same long avenue has different names in its different parts; for instance, the one long street running through the city from the Plaza by the Cathedral is named Calle de Plateros, Calle Profesa, Calle St. Francisco, etc. It is so with the streets parallel to this one, and the streets at right angles with these change their names at every corner."

"Oh, dear," said Miss Lejeune, "I cannot be bothered with so many names. I shall call this long street San Francisco street through all its length."

"Very well," said Tom; "as we shall always know what you are talking about, that will answer every purpose. Here is the Alameda, you see, that long pretty park we were in one day, coming back from the American Consulate."

"Oh, yes; so that is on San Francisco street!"

"Well, yes, only it is called something else; and the street at the end of the Alameda is San Diego street."

"Name me no more names," said Miss Augusta; "my best way is to never go out by myself, and then you can show me the way."

"You dear thing!" cried Bessie, "it is not half so puzzling as Paris, or Seville, or for the matter of that, your beloved Boston."

"I never can understand straight streets," replied Miss Augusta, somewhat pettishly; "it is just the same with Philadelphia, the hardest place I ever was in to find your way about in. In Boston you can remember the direction because it is so nice and crooked, and Paris is just the same in the old part."

She left the room as she said this, to prepare for going out.

"Bessie," said Tom, after she had closed the door, approaching his sister and speaking in a low, mysterious voice, "do not you think aunt Dut is getting a little shaky?"

"Hush, Tom!" cried Bessie indignantly; "are not you ashamed of yourself!"

The fire in Bessie's eye was such that Tom was alarmed, and looked about him for means to escape her wrath. A diversion was furnished him by a tap at the door which revealed a gentleman and lady standing on the threshold.

"Mr. March!" cried Bessie.

"Hallo, old fellow!" cried Tom.

"So you have really got to Mexico!" said the gentleman, cordially shaking hands.

"Yes; and where have you been all this time?"

"I have but this instant, so to speak, returned from Guadalajara."

"And we from Morelia," said the others; and then there ensued a voluble exchange of experiences, interrupted by an introduction of Miss Lejeune to the new-comers.

The Marches were chance acquaintances of Tom and Bessie, who had travelled with them a few days on their way to Mexico. The acquaintance was likely to grow into a permanent friendship, for they were charming people,—a Bohemian pair, according to the best sense of the term; that is, they believed in seeking and enjoying the best things the world can give, while dispensing with the superfluities of life. They were capital travellers, and having fallen in love with Mexico as soon as they saw it, were just ending their second winter there.

When the Horners first met them, they were returned from a brief trip to the North.

"We were just showing Miss Lejeune the plan of the city," said Tom, "for now we are going to do it up thoroughly. You are just the people to tell us where to begin."

"It is very easy to form a plan where to begin, but to say where to leave off is more difficult. Come and walk through the Portales now, unless you have some more serious plan on hand." Mr. March said this.

The side entrance of the Café Anglais, with a straight stairway leading directly to the corridor on which the Horners' rooms opened, is on a street which at a little distance becomes one of the portales, where the second story, jutting out over the sidewalk, and supported by arches, makes a covered way, all littered, so to speak, with booths and things to sell and buy.

"The Raymond excursionists," said Mr. March, "have spoiled the portales, by putting up the prices of everything. These fellows now expect a *peso* for what they once would have let you have for a few cents."

They stopped before a strange collection of things around which a little knot of people was gathered watching a bargain between the vendor and a wary purchaser. The Mexicans love this bargaining as the Arabs do; it is a sort of exercise of wit and cunning between the parties, like a game; the spectators follow the moves, amused to see the result on either side. The price asked in the beginning is always put too high, that it may be beaten down; the result agreed upon is generally much less than the seller proposed, and a little more than he expected; perhaps much less than the buyer expected, but a little more than he had meant to pay.

As they were moving along, amused by watching the crowd as well as their traffic of odds and ends, a brown man thrust before their eyes a scarf-pin, made of an opal set in cheap gilt. Opals are very plenty in Mexico, some of them valuable in quality.

"I wonder if I can have that," said Miss Lejeune; "does it cost much?"

Mr. March stopped, and asked the price in Spanish. The man said a dollar and a half, but in the same minute accepted twenty-five cents, which Mr. March offered him with no other argument than a shrug of the shoulders. The pin was transferred to his hands, and he passed it over to Miss Lejeune, saying,

"It is more than it is worth."

"I only want it as a specimen," said Miss Lejeune, "to carry home. Perhaps now I am unwise, for I fear opals, they are so very unlucky."

"Do not fear this on that account," said Mrs. March. "I doubt if it is enough of an opal to be unlucky."

Nevertheless Miss Lejeune took it home, and thought it very pretty. With its changing lights, and varying surface sometimes dull and sometimes brilliant, it kept up the character of a real opal, without bringing any ill luck.

They bought wax matches with double heads, that scratch at both ends. The thrifty Mexican defies the proverb about burning his candle at both ends, and having lighted his match once puts it carefully away under the lid of the box to use the other end next time, as it too is furnished with lighting power.

When they came to the large square before the Cathedral, the party decided to go on further and search for serapes. "We keep putting off buying them," said Miss Lejeune, "so long that I begin to think we shall go away without them. There were beauties in Morelia, but at first we scorned them, thinking we should do better at San Miguel."

"You can get perfectly good ones here," said Mr. March, and so they did, but not without a long search. The gaudy coal-tar colors lately introduced everywhere as dyes, have caught the fancy of the Mexican Indians, and their work now is invaded by the harsh, strong tints of magenta and other fierce colors. The shopmen could not understand why these customers turned away with a shudder from bright magenta and green stripes on scarlet, which they considered the very latest touch of fashion.

There were still to be found lovely white ones with black borders and black diamond-shaped centers spotted and marked with other colors, and darker ones with truly barbaric taste in decoration. Scrapes make admirable summer wraps, light coverings for piazza chairs, or portières. A wholesome fear of the Custom House prevented the Horners from buying many. Those they took home proved so popular that they wished they had brought dozens more.

CASTLE OF CHAPULTEPEC.

CHAPTER XXIV.

CHAPULTEPEC.

IT was drawing near the end of April, and signs of the wet season were approaching, although it was not time for rain to set in steadily. Every afternoon clouds came over the sky, as if a thunder-storm was approaching, and sometimes a few swift drops fell. Perhaps the whole afternoon was overcast, but then at sunset the sky was bright again with broad glimpses of a radiant heaven over the housetops and through the narrow street. Sometimes the rain poured down in a pelting shower, stopping as suddenly as it began. Altogether the latter part of the day had become uncertain, very different from the earlier winter, when fair weather was to be steadily relied upon; the travellers resolved to do their sight-seeing in the morning, when as yet it was always clear, cool and brilliant.

So one day an open carriage was waiting before the door of the Café Anglais as early as eight o'clock. Soon after, Miss Lejeune and Bessie come down the cork screw stairway and entered the low seat behind, while Tom climbed up with the Mexican driver.

"You ought to be up here to shrive this man properly," he said, as he turned back to look down on the ladies.

"You can do it perfectly well," said Bessie.

"Remember your Meisterschaft and begin every sentence with *quiere usted*, and the words will come to you."

"*Quiere usted*," in Spanish, answers to *vondez-vous* in French, and is a neat and polite way of beginning a question.

"My words may come to me, but his words will too," groaned Tom, "in a cataract, and I shall not understand one of them."

They were going to Chapultepec, armed with a pass, which is very important, if one wishes to see everything.

They drove through San Francisco street, past the great Iturbide Hotel, which was once the palace of the Emperor Augustin, past the Moorish tiled house and the handsome offices of the Central Railroad, then along the side of the long Alameda, heavily shaded by old trees, where children were already strolling with their nurses, and so on to the broad Paseo which leads to Chapultepec, broad, modern and well-paved, so that the carriage rolled easily over it and the horses' feet made a pleasant click on the solid road-bed.

"Does not this remind you of the Paseo in Madrid?" asked Miss Lejeune, from behind her parasol, as she leaned comfortably back in the carriage.

"Yes, somewhat," said Bessie, "but after all I seldom think of Spain now I am in Mexico. These American airs have whiffed away all the solemnity of Castile."

The avenue they were in was constructed by Maximilian. The promenade at the side is lined with stone-seats. At the entrance is a statue of Charles the Fourth, King of Spain from 1788 to 1808, a sovereign whose lawless reign destroyed in a few years the prosperity his country had reached under his predecessors, and made the way smooth for the inroads of Napoleon. It is doubtful whether a Mexican population would of its own accord erect a monument to such a king; it was made by the order of the viceroy who owed his appointment to King Charles. This was the Marquis de Branciforte, an Italian, and a near relative of the powerful favorite Godoy. The statue is large and imposing, and forms a fine ornament to the entrance of the Paseo, and so this worthless monarch rides in state, while few inquire his claim to such a position.

Columbus occupies the next *rond-point*, or circle, then come

Guatemozin, the last of the Aztec Emperors, and Juarez, three times President of the Mexican Republic.

It is about two miles to Chapultepec. Well outside the streets, the country stretched away in broad cultivated plains beyond which are glimpses of the volcanoes, Popocatepetl and Istaccihuatl, so often, however, veiled at that season that Miss Lejeune up to this very day pretended to believe there were no such mountains. The long line of the old aqueduct bringing water to the city appeared; the arches are not so graceful, nor is the color of the stone so warm as those of Morelia. It was a lovely drive, the dew yet sparkling on the grass, the air sweet and perfumed. They met one or two acquaintances on horseback returning from an early morning excursion through the avenues around the palace; a favorite habit with lovers of exercise and nature in Mexico.

And now the carriage passed through the gates and under the dark, solemn branches of huge cypress tress, driving slowly through the sombre avenues. It is a strange, weird place, haunted by the traditions of the Aztec monarchs who dwelt there. The trees are huge, and old, very old; long gray Spanish moss trails from the branches, it is silent, lonely and dim, except where through the long vistas bright sunshine gleams upon remote meadows.

Here, upon the royal hill of Chapultepec, was the most luxurious residence of the last of the Montezumas, consecrated too by the ashes of his ancestors. His gardens stretched for miles around the base of the hill. Two statues, one of himself, the other of his father, cut in *bas-relief* in the rock, endured until the middle of the last century. The great trees with trunks now more than fifteen feet in diameter were centuries old at the time of the conquest. These trees, *Ahuahuetes*, or "lords of the water," as they are called in Mexico, are themselves like solemn monuments of the past.

On the top of the lofty rock is a castle not existing in the time of the Montezumas. It was built at the close of the seventeenth century, by the Spanish Viceroy Galvez, to enhance the grandeur of his state, but he and his pretensions have disappeared like the greater ones of the Aztec monarchs. His presumption excited the jealousy of the Spanish Government, after they had been called upon to expend thousands of dollars upon the building, for the castle was a strong one, well adapted for a fortress, and he was suspected of making a stronghold for himself of it. It served as such for the Mexicans in their war with the United States when it was stormed by the Americans under General Scott in 1847. Meanwhile the pleasure apartments of the Spanish Viceroy fell to decay, neglected and exposed to the winds that beat about so elevated an exposure, and thus they remained until the Emperor Maximilian fixed his eyes too upon the picturesque spot, as a suitable one for his summer palace. During his brief reign he began decorating the chambers after the fashion of Pompeii, and building hanging gardens upon the terraces of the rock. After his fall, decay came upon it again.

Now workmen are once more busy in the lofty apartments, making them ready as a country seat for General Diaz, the present President of the Republic.

"I wonder," said Miss Lejeune, as they drove under the solemn archways made by over-reaching branches, "that he is not afraid to risk the fate which hangs over the Castle of Chapultepec,— so many unlucky dynasties have sought to revel on this spot."

"It is a temptation, every time," said Tom, "for the position is so lovely."

"I should like to be here in the evening," said Bessie.

"What! and meet all the ghosts that doubtless wander here!" exclaimed Miss Augusta.

"Yes, exactly that," she replied; "think what stores of information I should get from them."

"A motley crowd," said Miss Lejeune. "Montezuma's melancholy shade,— fancy him meeting Maximilian here!"

"They say that Doña Marina walks here," said Bessie, "but I should think she would be afraid of coming across Montezuma."

"The vice-regal wife of Galvez was celebrated for her beauty and goodness, perhaps she hovers around also," said Tom.

Such fancies were too gloomy for the early morning, and as they emerged from the shadow to ascend to the summit, the fine view bathed in sunshine chased away these ghosts.

The fortress is now occupied by a National Military School, something like West Point, where young Mexicans are studying to become soldiers. Military forms are observed at the entrance, but an all-powerful pass permitted the Horners to enter, and a polite young cadet, with some little English, and profuse Spanish, showed them about the rooms, decorated and deserted by Maximilian, now in process of preparation for Diaz.

The sight that claimed their whole attention, however, was the superb view from the elevated terrace, a broad platform with a parapet of stone. Far below them stretched the level valley bounded by the grand volcanoes, and in its place lay the City of Mexico spread out like a map, the straight avenues leading to it well defined by trees, domes and spires dominating over the flat-roofed houses about them. They hung over the balustrade a long time, studying the scene spread before them, and gathering for the first time just impressions of the breadth of the plateau encircled by its rampart of lofty mountains.

It is an enchanting spot, and as they took their seats again in the carriage, they all admitted that it was worth tempting the enmity of Fate, to live in such a superb situation.

They drove home so delighted with their morning at Chapultepec, that they resolved to undertake nothing more that day, a decision which was acted upon. In the evening they went to a theatre in the neighborhood where they were much amused by a modern play well rendered by the very theatrical troupe which had come with them on the steamer from Havana.

As the three entered the hotel after the performance, all sleepy and silent, they were met by François at the head of the staircase leading from the side-door, who remarked simply:

"*Les enfants sont revenus.*"

"*Les enfants!* what *enfants?*" demanded Miss Lejeune, as she burst open their door, of which the key hung in the outside.

There sat Helena and Jack primly perched on two chairs, looking rather frightened, very tired and miserable.

"What has happened!" exclaimed all the others in a breath.

The two children lifted up their voices and wept.

It was not a very cordial reception, to be sure.

CHAPTER XXV.

SANTA ANNA.

A LETTER from Mr. Johnstone, which the children brought with them, explained, better than their embarrassed and often interrupted statements, the reason of their return. The party, consisting of themselves and their parents, Minton and the baby, reached Orizaba in safety, where they were to stop over to break the journey down to Vera Cruz. There they met a party of English people coming up from the last steamer, who gave such frightful accounts of yellow fever in the *tierra caliente* that Mrs. Johnstone was fairly terrified. They said that Vera Cruz was intolerably hot, and that people were swarming from it to the steamers, which thus became themselves dangerous, as it was perfectly possible that cases of yellow fever might be among their passengers. Even a night in an infected hotel was pronounced dangerous.

"Oh! why did we not come sooner?" cried Mrs. Johnstone.

The children said it was terrible to see mamma, and papa did not know what to do. He walked up and down the room, and gnawed his mustache.

Finally the English people said they would bring the children back to Mexico, and they urged Mrs. Johnstone to come with them, but she could not bear to be again separated from her husband; and so after much worry and discussion, it was resolved that all of them should go on except Jack and Helena, and that they should return to the Horners.

"Papa said,— papa said," sobbed Helena, "that so he would not have all his eggs in one basket!"

"And so you came back to us," said Miss Lejeune, soothingly, "and we were all away, that was too bad. What became of the people who brought you, and what was their name?"

"Their name was Jones, and they went to the Chickabiddy!" said Helena, with a new burst of tears.

This frivolous name had been bestowed upon the Iturbide Hotel by Tom in a careless moment.

"Well, well," said Bessie, in her cheeriest tones, "do not cry; it is very nice you have come back, for we were becoming so grown-up there was no living with us. We wanted some children very badly, in order to improve their minds, for only think, we went to Chapultepec to-day, and there was nobody to tell the history of it to, for everybody knew just the same as everybody else."

So Helena's eyes were dried, and just then some cold chicken was brought up on a tray, for the poor things had been quite starved all the evening. The good-natured Horners and Miss Lejeune put aside their own feelings and set themselves to cheer up the poor little wanderers, soon rewarded by returning smiles, and a happy flow of talk from Jack, who at the beginning had been as silent as a moulting canary.

"It is a great deal nicer to be with you," he said, his mouth full of drum-stick, "and papa told us to tell you not to worry about them, for he did not believe half they said about the yellow fever."

It proved, indeed, that the alarm of the English people was only a scare, such as seizes upon travellers with but small occasion. The parent Johnstones found Vera Cruz remarkably cool, and heard nothing of any contagion either ashore or on the ship. They reached Progreso in perfect safety, their voyage only disturbed by Mrs. Johnstone's anxiety for her absent children, and her vain speculations as to what would become of them, and how they would ever be brought back to her. This indeed was one of the problems left for time to unfold.

The Horners cheerfully resumed their burden.

"We have had our Sunday out," remarked Tom, "and now work begins again."

The very next morning he went to Chapultepec again with Jack, going over the same ground, and more than the same. He found he enjoyed the trip himself still more than the first; indeed there is a charm about the place which increases with every visit, so that foreigners living in the City of Mexico find themselves repeatedly returning to Chapultepec, instead of visiting other spots in the suburbs.

The leader of the revolution which deposed the Emperor Augustin Iturbide, was Antonio Lopez de Santa Anna, who for many years afterward took a leading part in Mexican affairs. He first came into public notice in 1821 in the war of Independence; the next year having expelled the royalists from Vera Cruz, he was appointed to the command of that city. He was, later, deposed by Iturbide, who had proclaimed himself emperor, but Santa Anna refused to submit to his authority, and succeeded in compassing his downfall. Revolutions followed each other in rapid succession, between Spaniards and Mexicans, matters being mixed up with all sorts of complications, among which the independence of Texas became a leading one. Texas, in the north of Mexico, and close to the United States, was settled by several thousand Americans,— as the inhabitants of the United States are still often called, to distinguish them from Mexicans. These Americans refused to submit to Santa Anna; the United States government took their part, and in time annexed Texas to their own country. Out of this grew a quarrel connected with the boundary line, and a war was begun which lasted from the end of 1845, till February, 1848, when it was closed by a treaty giving New Mexico and California also to the United States.

It was in this war that General Taylor became famous, who was afterwards President of the United States. The Mexicans were constantly defeated, although they fought with the greatest bravery. General Scott captured the City of Mexico on September 14, 1847, after storming the castle at Chapultepec the day before.

At the time of the assault there were in it many officers of rank, besides all the students of the military academy. General Bravo, with a picked force of Mexicans, held the position. He was considered one of the ablest of the Mexican officers, to whom it was safe to entrust so great a responsibility. Santa Anna, with the chief mass of the Mexican army, was in the City of Mexico, in full communication with the castle.

An old powder-mill in the rear, called Molino del Rey, was first attacked, and after two days the Castle height itself was stormed and scaled. The Mexicans were driven from their defences after a short resistance, and the American flag floated from the ramparts.

The cheers of the victors were distinctly heard in Mexico, and an ominous cessation of firing gave notice to Santa Anna that Chapultepec had fallen and that the war was ended.

After peace was restored with the United States, Santa Anna was forced to retire; expressing a wish to seek in a foreign land the calm which he failed to find in that of his birth, he was permitted to leave the country. But in a few years he returned to Mexico and was received with enthusiasm, and made President again. He sought to elevate himself to the position of a despot, and again was forced to abdicate. He is generally regarded as the ablest of the Mexican generals; like Iturbide, his ambition was his ruin; he was governed by no loyal patriotism, but a personal thirst for power. He was five times President, always turning up again, after abdicating, like the great actors who are continually making their farewell appearance. He re-appeared in 1864, and professed his adhesion to the Emperor Maximilian, but he was dismissed and retired, living, however, several years longer. Santa Anna was born in 1798, and died June 20, 1876.

CYPRESS GROVES OF CHAPULTEPEC, IN THE TIME OF MAXIMILIAN.

When Madame Calderon first arrived in Mexico, in 1839, she visited him at his country house not far from Vera Cruz. In her delightful journal she describes him as a gentlemanly, good-looking, rather melancholy-looking person, with a sallow complexion, fine dark eyes and an interesting expression. He had already lost a leg in the course of a war with France; even then he expressed his intentions of living in retirement, having had enough of the world's prizes and defeats; yet this was but the middle of his career. He had already been twice President, and was to fill that office three times more.

Jack was very much interested in all these matters, which Tom took pains to tell him about, as they walked through the lovely avenues of ancient trees. Not far from the steep ascent to the castle they saw the stone monument erected in memory of the heroes on the Mexican side of the war of 1847.

"You cannot think," said Jack, "how glad I am to come back. As we were going off down to Vera Cruz I was wondering how I should ever find out all the rest about Cortés after he reached the City of Mexico. Papa said he would show me Prescott's Conquest of Mexico, but I should not know what to skip if Bessie was not there."

"I do not believe you would want to skip anything," said Tom, "after you had once begun it; but it is rather a big book for a boy of your size, and to tell you the truth, I never read it myself till the other day. We must persuade Bessie to go on with Cortés and his adventures, and then we can go and see the tree of the *Noche Triste* and whatever else is left to show the traces of the *Conquistadores*."

"I thought you might be sorry to have us back," said Jack, in a sheepish tone, with his head on one side. "At first I told papa I would not come, because it would be such a bother."

"What made you think that?" demanded Tom, with a slight sense of guilt.

"Well, you know that day at Morelia, when the letters came" — Tom remembered that he had not been over careful to conceal his vexations that day.

"Papa felt awfully, I expect," said Jack. "He told me he wished he had never accepted the appointment to Merida; he said that if it was not for such kindness as you and Miss Lejeune showed us, he did not know where we should all be. He was going to write you more, but he had to be fanning poor mamma."

Tom smiled, sighed, then laughed, saying, "It's all right, old fellow, so don't fret about it."

CHAPTER XXVI.

THE DEATH OF MONTEZUMA.

WHILE Tom and Jack were at Chapultepec that morning, Bessie took Helena to some baths on the Paseo. They all drove out of town together, squeezed up in a small cab, and while the boys went on to the castle, the girls were left at a corner where a long sign on some low rambling buildings advertised the

BAÑOS DE ROSARIO.

They passed through a gateway into a little office with a counter, where tickets were given them in exchange for a moderate sum, and then, following a loosely clad *muchacho* across the usual garden, they were shown into the bath. It was an immense high place, lighted only from the top, and when the high double door was closed upon them, and Bessie had drawn a huge bolt inside to secure it, they felt somewhat solemn, for all was still within except a sound of rushing water, although in the distance they heard splashing and the laughter of other bathers in other rooms like this one. The floor was brick, the whole space being occupied with a round swimming-place twelve or fifteen feet across, except a walk two or three feet around it. The edge of the bath was higher on one side than the other, so that running water, coming into the bottom of the bath, while it kept it constantly full, was constantly flowing over the lower margin, where it ran off through a sort of trough. In a moderately dry corner, stood a dressing table with a glass over it, covered with the usual bath implements. There were a couple of chairs by it, with matting in front of them for the feet. In the opposite corner was a shower-bath, and in the space between, the clear green reservoir of fresh water, about four feet deep, with a smooth bottom of red brick. It was most inviting. Bessie, scorning the steps, had soon plunged in, and was swimming about joyfully in the mild soft water. Helena more cautiously descended the steps and found the water just up to her chin. When they were refreshed, rubbed and dressed, they came out again into the office. Bessie thought she was to return the torn-off scraps of yellow tickets which the *muchacho* had given back to her, but a chorus of assistants exclaimed that these were good for a return ride to the city.

They stood waiting in the sunny gateway for the car, and made friends with a French woman drying her long hair, who was also waiting with her two children. Bessie enjoyed talking in good easy French as a change from the thorny paths of unpractised Spanish. She found it much easier to be polite in French, for although Spanish abounds in terms of compliment, she had not yet much skill in using them. By and by a gentleman came along, who was presented by the French lady; he insisted on treating the whole company to little cakes which were produced from a glass-case in the office, and furnished by the bath-keeper. Bessie did not know very well what to do. She did not much like to accept these delicacies, while to refuse seemed ungracious. Helena's wistful eyes decided the question, and she allowed the little girl to take one of the cakes. Afterwards she drew out her purse to pay her share of this refection; this was forbidden by the effusive Spaniard, and the French woman said in a low tone, "Put up your purse, he will not allow it," but Bessie insisted.

All this seemed like a strange dream, and Bessie was beginning to feel uncomfortable. Luckily the car arrived just then, and all hands entered it. They went back to town by a route wholly unknown to them, and when the new friends stopped the

THE DEATH OF MONTEZUMA.

car for them at a point they considered nearest the Café Anglais, Bessie stood for a few moments wondering where to go next. A short walk brought them to some trees she thought familiar, and at the next four corners where the streets crossed, she perceived to her joy Miss Lejeune, hanging over a balcony.

"Why!" exclaimed Helena, "is this our house?"

"I never should have thought it," replied Bessie, "but so it seems. And there are Jack and Tom!"

These two were approaching from the other direction, having walked all the way from Chapultepec, tired enough and quite ready for luncheon. The Marches joined them, much amazed to find the little Johnstones in the party. There was a great deal of talk and merry jesting in the course of the meal.

This took place in a side room of the restaurant, under the very spot where Helena had passed the first night in the inside chamber.

"That was your *Noche Triste*," said Bessie.

"Tell us now about that," said Jack, as he helped himself to strawberries brought by Jules to his elbow.

"Wait till we have finished coffee," said Bessie, "and then the rest can go away if they like." They decided later to go back to the balcony in the large room before she began to talk.

"Let me see, where was I?" she asked. "It is so long since we have had anything to do with Cortés. The Spaniards lived in clover in Mexico, in the palace Montezuma lent them; but the first thing Cortés did was to seize the king and make a prisoner of him in that palace. It seems strange the Aztecs allowed this, but they did, and Montezuma was weak and gentle, and Cortés got him to say that it was all right. Still, Cortés was no nearer to the possession of Mexico than at first, and he grew rather nervous about that. He had to go away too, down to the coast to deal with a powerful armament sent from Cuba to seize him as a rebel.

"He left Mexico in charge of Alvarado, one of his captains in whom he had great faith; but who was neither so wise nor so patient as Cortés. During his absence, at a religious festival of the Aztec nobles, Alvarado fell upon them with his men and killed them every one. They had come without weapons, all dressed in their feast costumes, made of feather work, ornamented with precious stones, and with gold bracelets on their arms and legs, thinking of nothing but a joyful celebration, so that they could not defend themselves, and were simply massacred.

"The tidings spread like wildfire. The hitherto inactive city rose in arms to a man, and the very next day the Spaniards were assaulted with fury, and besieged in their garrison.

"When Cortés returned, he found his army shut up in the palace of Ayaxacatl, which Montezuma had given them, suffering for food and water. The whole Mexican population were roused against him, and a storm gathering which would be fearful to resist.

"Cortés at length resolved to have Montezuma address his people from the walls, to tell them that if a way were opened for them, the Spaniards would depart and trouble them no more. The Aztec monarch, in his imperial robes, ascended to the roof. As soon as he was seen there was silence amid the thousands of armed men gathered before the palace, but suddenly the tumults burst forth again, and he was struck to the ground by one of the stones hurled at him by his own infuriated people. The attack was continued, and the cry could be heard, 'the bridges are broken down! Not one of you shall escape.'

"The next day, poor old Montezuma died. His wound, though serious, might not have proved mortal, but he refused all remedies, and tore off the bandages applied to it. He had survived his honor, he had lost the reverence of his people, and he no longer wished to live.

"Before he died he commended his children to the care of

THE DEATH OF MONTEZUMA.

Cortés, and to the interest of his master, the Emperor, saying, 'Your Lord will do this for the love I have shown the Spaniards, — though it has brought me to this condition.'

"On the thirtieth of June, 1520, he expired in the arms of a few of his nobles, who still faithfully attended him. With him terminated practically the royal line of the Aztecs, and the glory passed away from their empire.

"At midnight on the first of July, 1520, the march began of the Spaniards escaping from the city. They had to leave behind much of the wealth they had collected from the Mexicans, but still soldiers were heavily weighted with gold and jewels they could not bear to abandon. They were not allowed to go unmolested. The whole city poured out upon them, and the lake was covered with boats filled with armed men. There was a drizzling rain, the night was cloudy, they had to press through the narrow streets, and cross the canals on which no bridges were left. The last of these was wide and deep. The horsemen plunged into the water, those on foot followed as best they could. Many of them weighted down with the treasure they loved so much, were buried with it in the bottom of the lake.

"Alvarado, when he came to the brink, paused a moment, then setting his long lance firmly on the bottom of the lake, he cleared the wide gap at one bound. The place is still called Alvarado's Leap. The Aztecs gazed with amazement at this feat. A little fragment of the army escaped from the town through an adjacent village, and Cortés, watching his draggled and decimated soldiers, a mere handful of them left, is said to have covered his face with his hands and wept. He was sitting under a tree when this happened, and this tree is still standing to mark the spot. It is called the tree of the *Noche Triste*, or sad night, and a sad night indeed it was. His army destroyed, most of his horses lost, as well as all his artillery, muskets and ammunition, his men frightened and discouraged, Cortés knew himself to be in the middle of a hostile land with scarcely the means of defending his personal safety. What a contrast with his proud hopes of conquering the whole country!"

"A sad night indeed!" said Tom, "and of course we must go and see the tree."

"Let us go now," said Mr. March, starting up. "Is there time?"

They consulted the time-tables, and decided to try it, although it was already nearly five o'clock in the afternoon. For a wonder, the clouds had passed off without rain, and there was promise of a brilliant sunset. So they all sallied forth to a tram-car.

CHAPTER XXVII.

"NOCHE TRISTE."

TAKING a car, on which was printed the difficult name Atzcapotzalco, in the square of the Cathedral, our party were soon rumbling over the very ground trampled by the unfortunate Spaniards on the night of their disastrous retreat from the city.

It is difficult to imagine it the same place. The ancient city was not only surrounded by the salt waters of Tezcoco Lake, but intersected by canals which flowed through every part of the city, now Mexico stands high and dry on the main land far away from the lake. The temple of the Aztec war-god is gone, and in its place stands the Cathedral. The great causeway which used to run nearly north and south, and the other one at right angles to it going east and west, are now paved streets, shod with iron for the track of the tram-car, with no trace of any deep canal where armed men could be drowned. As the Horners' car thumped and bumped over an uneven crossing they were told by a Yankee passenger that "he guessed that was the leap of Alvarado." The solid arches of the aqueduct run for a distance parallel with the track, a stately fountain with quaint carvings standing at one end of the row. Outside of the heart of the city, the road somewhat resembles the ancient Causeway, with a stagnant ditch on either side, for the surrounding region is lower, although not recalling at all the broad lagoon beset with canoes full of angry Indians.

The tree is in the suburb of Popotla. It is another of the *ahuehuetes* like those at Chapultepec, but the poor thing has been so maltreated that it has none of the dignity of those huge creatures. There is a large cavity in the trunk, made, it is said, by some picnic party who kindled a fire to boil their kettle with, not many years ago, and forgot to put it out. The embers smouldered for many a day, and the heat creeping up within the ancient bark charred and hollowed the trunk. This is sufficient to account for bare branches above, and it is a wonder that any

DISTANT VIEW OF MEXICO.

life remains to the rest. Its forlorn unflourishing condition suits its history better than luxuriant growth would have done.

A stone wall protects the tree from the possible danger of future fires to boil the kettles of other picnics, and the graceful belfry of a church close by should comfort the ghosts of the *Conquistadores* if they haunt the spot, for the cross on its summit is convincing proof of their ultimate triumph over their heathen enemies.

It was sunset by the time the Horners arrived at the tree. The

THE TREE OF THE NOCHE TRISTE.

car, after they left it, rattled off towards its destination with the difficult name, and they remained alone with their traditions of the Sad Night.

The suburb was lonely and silent. Not far off a row of slender eucalyptus trees bent and moaned in the wind which was rising. A bank of thunder-clouds behind the little church brought into full relief its white outline.

The children stared at the tree, the elders were silent, following the story of the flight, and fancying the dejection of Cortés, as he counted over his diminished band. It was to them, then, a very

FOUNTAIN OF THE AQUEDUCT.

real piece of history. Somehow, the battered old tree brought it much nearer to them than all the written accounts they had read.

"Poor old Cortés," said Miss Lejeune at length, "how provoked he must have been with Alvarado, who had brought all this upon him."

"He could not say anything, either," said Bessie, "when Alvarado was coming off so bravely."

"It was no time for quarrelling," said Tom, "and I dare say they were too tired and hungry even to be cross."

"By the way," said Mr. March, "I am sorry to say I am hungry; where is our car?"

They had to wait some time longer, and their romance had vanished with the fading lights, before their conveyance was heard in the far distance. It was pretty dark, and somewhat chilly. The children were restless. Bessie found in the pocket of her little rough coat one very small and ancient biscuit which was divided between them. This appeased the small people for a time, but every one was glad to climb into the car, spite of a strong perfume of kerosene from its lamp. They all forgot to take a last glimpse of the tree, and nobody ever mentioned Cortés all the way back to the hotel. They were all planning what they would have for dinner, and as soon as they reached the café, they summoned Jules to bring them something good, and hot, at once. It was nearly eight o'clock, — very late for the children's dinner, — but it was a jolly one, and they all slept the better for it.

It is at this darkest moment of the career of Cortés, that he first gains our sympathy. Up to this time, it may be he has appeared only a bold adventurer seeking excitement, glory and plunder, in an unequal combat with an uncivilized people, gaining easy victories through the advantages he possessed in arms and skill.

Now that he has lost all, and sits discouraged under the cypress, we have to feel sorry for him, and, in the sequel, must admire the heroism which enabled him to face the situation, — the patience, tact and endurance which will extricate him and his followers from the depths of failure, and lead them back to success.

He had returned from Vera Cruz triumphant, after overcoming the band sent to disconcert him by the Governor of Cuba, had taken possession of the ammunition that party had brought against him, and by power or persuasion, added to his own forces those who had come to destroy him. Thus on his return to the capital, he took with him about a thousand foot-soldiers, and one hundred horse, an important addition to those he had left behind. That these should be brought only to be swept away with the rest of his army was a bitter element in the misfortune, which he had to face, when he was forced to reckon his losses.

The ammunition and beautiful little train of artillery with which he had entered the city were gone. Not a musket remained, for they had all been thrown away, in the eagerness of the men to escape; only their swords and a few damaged cross-bows were left. The cavalry was reduced to twenty-three horses. The greater part of the treasure, baggage, papers, all were lost in the water.

But Cortés could not remain inactive. The Mexicans, busy in clearing the streets of the dead, and themselves in a bad plight after the battle, were not heard of during the day following the *Noche Triste*, but Cortés knew well this could not last, and at midnight with his little band he marched away round the northern side of the lake, keeping at a safe distance from the capital.

His soldiers were nearly starving, with little to eat but wild cherries which they found on the roadside, or a few ears of corn left in the fields unplucked. For seven days they journeyed in this way, during which Cortés was wonderfully serene and cheerful, hiding his own sufferings, encouraging his men. Then they came to a place where they were obliged to give battle to a huge army composed of levies from all the surrounding country, collected by Cuitlahuac, the brother and successor of Montezuma, a brave warrior and skilful general.

It was under his orders that the terrible attack of the *Noche Triste* had been carried forward; he was declared king, and upon his hasty coronation, the Spanish prisoners taken in the fatal rout of July 1, were sacrificed alive.

This battle at Otumba was fought on the eighth of July, 1520, against fearful odds; the little band of Spaniards were aided by the Tlascalan allies, who were fighting almost in sight of their homes, and strove to cut their way through the Aztec army, with but little hope of safety.

Suddenly in the thick of battle, Cortés saw the chief of the opposing army borne upon a litter, surrounded by a body of young warriors, the flower of the Indian nobles, in gay and ornamented costume. Cihuaca, the chief, was dressed in beautiful feather-work, with a splendid tuft of plumes set in gold and precious stones on his head. The Spanish commander, relentless of this childish display, pointed out the group, crying, "There is our mark! Follow me!" In a few moments they were close to the chief, and Cortés himself struck him to the ground with his lance. A panic ensued, the guards fled, and with them all the Indian army, trampling each other down in their confusion, and leaving heaps of booty on the field.

The Spaniards were thus enabled to enter Tlascala with a show of victory, although it was with doubtful hearts, for they were returning with crippled forces, to bring desolation and mourning to the friends of the allies who had gone forth expecting to overcome their enemies, the Mexicans. The old chief of the Tlascalans came out to meet them, cordially showing them the greatest sympathy for their losses. The general and his suite were lodged in the palace of this friendly chieftain, and there they stayed several weeks, to rest and recover from their fatigue and many wounds. Cortés himself had lost two fingers of the left hand, and besides, a fever came upon him, so that the great hero lay stretched in bed for several days.

He was soon well again, and plotting, with characteristic elasticity, how to regain the ground he had lost, never thinking for an instant of giving up the Conquest of Mexico.

AN ANCIENT VAIL HOUSE.

CHAPTER XXVIII.

MAYAN CITIES.

IN due time letters came from the Johnstones, — mamma's as usual written in a plaintive tone, yearning for her dear children, and regretting that she saw but little of dear papa, with no clear account of the manner of life she was leading in Merida.

From Mr. Johnstone, Tom received a cordial, manly letter full of confidence in the patience of his friends, and containing practical references to money matters, calculated to make easy the mind of the young guardian thus suddenly called upon to continue his care of two irresponsible children. Mr. Johnstone's letter to Jack was filled with accounts of the antiquities of Yucatan which he had already begun to examine ; and from this time forward, the children heard but little of the actual life of their parents, and a great deal of the manners and customs of the ancient Mayans. Mr. Johnstone's diplomatic duties amounted to little or nothing, and he began at once to make prolonged absences from home, visiting the mines in the neighborhood, or at greater distances, leaving the small household to run itself.

Miss Lejeune and Bessie often wondered how it was managed. They guessed that the nurse looked after affairs, for Mrs. Johnstone had evidently lapsed into a sort of invalid languor which prevented her knowing or caring what there was for dinner. She spoke once or twice of their native Mayan maid as neat and tidy, but inefficient, confessing that she herself had been but once in the kitchen belonging to their establishment.

"I wonder," said Bessie confidentially, one day after the reading

of the letters, "whether they really do have anything to eat."
"If Mr. Johnstone is away so much, it does not much signify," said Tom. "I am glad you are not with them, aunt Augusta!"
"So am I, thankful!" she exclaimed. "I might be constrained to go into the kitchen and cook something for myself!"
"Poor old nurse," murmured Bessie, "at any rate, she is spared the care of Jack and Helena."

As Jack and Helena were perfectly happy, and as they made a pleasant element in the present Horner circle, everything worked well. They showed a surprising indifference to the manners and customs of the ancient Mayans, but a strong interest in the habits and pursuits of the modern Horners: thus both branches of the Johnstone family were content with their lot.

The elders, however, were greatly interested in all Mr. Johnstone wrote about the remains of ancient cities which abound in Yucatan. The country is covered with them, and after visiting those which are well-known, Jack's father hoped to explore others for himself, about which there is yet much to discover. The Mayans, as we have said, are supposed to have descended from the same great stock as the other early settlers of Mexico; but their separation from the different Nahua nations must have taken place long before the time of the *Conquistadores*.

They established a great flourishing empire on the shores of the Gulf of Mexico; which extended in its day over the greater part of Central America.

The first expedition of Mr. Johnstone was to Uxmal, the most examined and explored of the ancient Mayan cities. There he saw the Casa del Gobernador. It is a large stone building, plain on the outside, profusely decorated inside, with carved arabesques of strange designs, of which it is hard to trace the meaning. There are figures looking something like elephants' trunks, which is remarkable, since no elephants have been known to exist in this country. It makes some people think that these early tribes had wandered from the East, and had the memory or tradition of elephants from Asia. But perhaps the carvings were not meant for elephants.

In another letter Mr. Johnstone described the ruins of Chichen-Itza, a city which has kept its ancient Mayan name; the ground there is strewed for several miles with overturned columns, broken sculpture, and masses of rubbish where once were noble buildings.

GOVERNOR'S HOUSE, UXMAL.

This city was one of the religious centres of Yucatan, and these are supposed to be the ruins of temples and sacred edifices.

The Horners thought the place must look like Karnak on the Nile, where columns and carvings are tumbled about in hopeless confusion. There is a good deal in the profile carvings on the stones of the mines of Central America like the Egyptian figures. We can understand better the story told by the Egyptian representations, because we have the key to their hieroglyphics. The Aztec-Mayan records are all in confusion, so many of their printed picture writings and other records were destroyed by the Spaniards in a mistaken zeal for their own religion, which made them think it was noble to do away with such heathen symbols. Explorers are now always hoping and longing to find some clue to the figures and carvings scattered in this profusion of destruction, which will tell us more about the early tribes than can now be known.

A statue found at Chichen-Itza is now in the Museum of Antiquities in Mexico. It represents Chac-Mool, the Tiger King, and this is the story about him: — He was married to a beautiful princess named Kinich Katmō, who was so beautiful that Aac, her husband's brother, fell in love with her, and killed her husband, so that he might marry her himself; but Kinich Katmō remained faithful to her murdered spouse, and had this statue made of him, and also ornamented her palace with paintings representing the principal scenes of his life and his sad death. This may have happened some time in the sixth century.

BAS-RELIEF AT CHICHEN-ITZA.

Having been made to listen to the story in their father's letter, the children looked with curiosity at the statue in the courtyard of the museum. It is larger than life. The head, larger than natural size, is adorned with a kind of crown, and two earrings, carved with hieroglyphics.

All these remains testify to the cultivation of the Mayans. Their number and size, the taste displayed in their ornament and the richness of it, must strike all who ever see them. Evidently these people understood weaving, embroidery, and every industrial art known to us, and there is no doubt that when the Spaniards arrived, the Indians were superior to them in such things. But Cortés had horses, powder, enterprise, and with such advantages he overpowered the poor Indians, and ruthlessly destroyed a civilization which he could not even appreciate.

"Dear me!" sighed Miss Lejeune; "how interesting it all is! and how Mr. Johnstone must enjoy it."

"You might go there instead of going home, and take the children back!" suggested Bessie.

"Oh, do! oh, do!" cried the children at once.

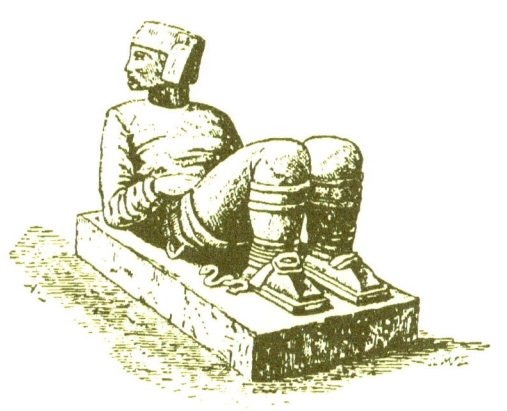

THE STATUE OF CHAC-MOOL.

"You must reflect, my friends," said Miss Lejeune, shaking her head, "that it is time for us to go home pretty soon. Look at my letters," she added, holding up a bunch of them, "every one of them demands what are my summer plans."

"Mamma also," said Bessie, "is growing very pressing; she wants to know what is to become of her this summer."

"It all depends, of course," said Tom with a laugh, "upon what little Miss Hervey intends to do."

This was the baby of the family, at present the only direct descendant of the Horners, whose travels have so long been described for the edification of young people. She was the daughter, scarce six months old, of Mary Horner, married to Clarence

Hervey, and the granddaughter of Mr. and Mrs. Horner, who now began to regard themselves as old people, and to concentrate their lives more and more on the happiness of the younger generation. Grandmamma and grandpapa were wholly devoted to the child, and had entirely merged their fondness for travel in their devotion to the nursery.

"When will little Mary begin her travels, I wonder," said Tom. "I wish she would order us all to Japan."

"It is too funny to have Clarence so settled down," said Bessie. "Mary writes she cannot induce him to make any plans for summer."

"I believe we shall all stay in New York," said Tom, "and help tend the baby. By the way, I bought a rattle for her ladyship this morning."

"You are just as devoted as all the rest of us!" cried Bessie.

Just then the Marches dropped in, and seeing all the letters lying about, they asked, "What are the plans?"

"There is but one plan," said Miss Lejeune vivaciously, starting from her seat. "We have all decided that we must go right home and see the baby."

"Home!" cried the Marches in dismay, "but we have just got another plan, and we want you to join us. It is to go to Guadalajara."

The Horners shouted with laughter, for the Marches were always going to Guadalajara.

"We really must go home," said Tom gravely. "My father writes rather impatiently, and it is high time we were off. But we will promise to come back for Guadalajara."

"And Patzcuaro," said Miss Lejeune.

"And Uruapan," added Bessie.

"And Manzanillo," concluded Tom, "for then I can go home by the way of Japan."

"You will persuade Mary to let you take the baby," said Bessie.

"And us too?" asked Helena.

PALENQUE.

CHAPTER XXIX.

NACHAN, — THE SEVEN SERPENTS.

IN a dense tropical forest, thickly overgrown with tangled vines and rank foliage, are the ruins of an immense city, — vast artificial terraces of cut stone, surmounted by solid buildings of one, two or three stories, carved with figures in relief. On great slabs of stone there are colossal figures resembling Grecian art more nearly than that of the East. The walls are covered with hieroglyphics to which there is as yet no key, offering a puzzle to antiquarians and explorers for which none can furnish a solution.

This was Nachan, the capital of a great and powerful empire, the Sacred City, the residence of the monarch, who was king and priest at once. The modern name for the place is Palemke, meaning "City of the Priests," a word often confounded with the Spanish word *Palenque*, a palisade.

This great city was already in ruins, its site forgotten, and buried in the wilderness, at the period of the Conquest. Cortés must have marched close to it once, when he was on his way to Honduras, after Mexico was fairly in his possession, but he makes no allusion to it, and it is probable that he had no notion of its existence. Cortés and his army groped about in the gloomy woods finding their way only with the compass and map, climbing the tallest trees to see about them on every side only an interminable forest. Had they suddenly come upon the traces of the ancient city, how excited they would have been! But they passed it by, unconscious; it was not discovered until 1750, more than two hundred years later.

The most interesting monument at Palemke is the so-called Temple of the Cross. From this two tablets have been removed, one to the Smithsonian Institute at Washington, and the other to the National Museum in Mexico. A third remains at Palemke.

Each of these tablets is six feet four inches in height, four feet wide, and six inches thick. The rock is of fine grain, and a rich cream color. They are covered with hieroglyphics, and the one in the Smithsonian may be fancied to represent the Christian Cross. It is on a pedestal surrounded by unknown characters. It cannot be doubted that the ornaments, signs and symbols of this complex carving have some especial significance, containing the interpretation of the meaning of the wonderful monument. But the interpretation has yet to be found, and we have only the guesses of antiquarians to explain them. It is surmised that the likeness to the Christian Cross is only accidental, and that the monument was dedicated to the Sun, as the great creative power, to the Year, as the producer of rains, and to Time as the controller of human destiny.

When this was first brought to light, it was thought to reveal the fact that the Christian faith had existed in this city discovered in the wilderness, and that it had been miraculously preserved there. The tablet containing the cross was carried off, but abandoned, no one knows why, in the depths of the forest which has overgrown the city. Here it was found by Americans, who took possession of it for their National Museum, and it was placed in the Smithsonian Collection at Washington.

It can hardly be doubted that more ruined cities lie hidden in these unexplored regions, perhaps containing in carving or statue signs plain enough to make a key to the enigma of those that are already known. They are seldom visited, it is so difficult to reach them. Not far from Copan, a little village with the reputation of growing good tobacco, are ruins so overgrown at the time of their discovery that the tangled vines had to be cut away with

TABLET IN THE TEMPLE OF THE CROSS.

the axe before they could be brought to light. Again the vines have closed over them, hiding the strange but ugly images once regarded as models of human skill and religious fervor.

Copan is near the boundary of Guatemala and Honduras, for the great Mayan race extended its power far into Central America, and traces of its monuments are found throughout the whole region.

Up to 1823, Guatemala, like Mexico, was governed by Viceroys from Spain. It was won for Spain by Alvarado, in 1524, and Charles the Fifth soon after appointed a captain-general for it. The people of Guatemala annexed themselves to the empire of Iturbide; upon his fall they became a part of the Central American Federal Republic, from which Guatemala has since seceded and proclaimed itself independent.

The children listened with a good deal of interest to Mr. Johnstone's description of the ruins he had seen and those he meant to see. He was evidently longing to be off for Palemke, Copan and the rest, restrained only by doubt about his family. The Horners could not help fancying that the excellent man would like them to originate some plan for the entertainment of his encumbrances, which would leave him free to pursue the ancient Mayans with all the ardor he had; they made merry over this idea, and from time to time asked each other if there was any scheme yet for the young Johnstones. Meanwhile they kept on sight-seeing in Mexico, as if that were the only thing on their minds, while Jack and Helena, with the irresponsibility of youth, thought everything was working splendidly.

One morning they passed on the canal, the Viga, as it is called, nobody knows just why.

"I thought it was the Vega," said Miss Lejeune. "Like the plain where Queen Isabella sat down."

"So did I," said Bessie, "but it is spelled with an *i*."

Tram-cars brought them to the edge of the canal, where they chose from a flock of boats, the one preferred by Mr. March. It

LEFT SIDE OF TABLET.

was of the hen-coop description, with two narrow seats running the length of the covered part. The flat bottom of the boat was a little more comfortable than the seat. A swarthy Indian, slightly draped in a white garment, stood up in the stern and poled them slowly up the broad wide canal. While still within city limits, the shores were bordered with tumbled-down buildings, picturesque arch-ways, overgrown with vines. Out of town, the broad stretching flat banks were planted with gardens, and at intervals they came to Indian villages which reminded the Horners of the Arab villages on the banks of the Nile. Traces are to be seen of the *chinampas*, or floating gardens, which so amazed the Spaniards, richly cultivated with flowers and vegetables, and then movable, like rafts, to different mooring-places. They have all anchored themselves now with roots fast growing in the soil, but the flowers are there, and the taste of the Indians for floral decoration is the same as that of their Aztec ancestors.

The canal was quiet when the Horners were there. Only a few boats floated up or down, lazily pushed by the monotonous movement of the pole. The morning was soft and hazy; a yellow light pervaded the air; the slowly changing

RIGHT SIDE OF TABLET.

scene, like a panorama, required close watching, so charming was each effect of reflection, color, form. A sort of melancholy came upon the party now observing the simple contented lives of the Indians, keeping up unconsciously the traditions of a great race, happy in the faithful fulfilment of their lowly routine, but lost wholly to the knowledge even of the existence to those predecessors, their pomp of living, their prominence among the races, their high place in the civilization of their time.

When they had reached the landing place on their return, the street-car they wanted was just starting. Shouts, whistles, waving handkerchiefs, these modern methods of stopping these essentially modern conveyances, were used in vain. Mr. March made a dumb signal to a little scion of the Aztecs who stood looking on, and he started after the car, running as fast as his little brown Aztec legs could carry him. The car was out of sight, and the party gave it up, walking without haste across the broad dusty thoroughfare, and over a bridge. At the turning of the street, they beheld their car patiently waiting, and the small Aztec panting beside it. The *cuartillo* that he loved was doubly given him, and the Horners' luncheon was saved, as well as the serenity of Jules, who liked his Americans best when they turned up on time. The sharp contrast of modern civilization upon Indian survivals, is constantly presenting itself in Mexico. It is more striking than in Spain, where, as Bessie expressed it, "there is less Yankee and more Hidalgo."

"Helena, my dear," said Bessie that evening as she was putting her to bed, "do you know what we have decided?"

"No," said Helena, "but I guess it is something nice."

"I hope you will think so," replied Bessie.

"Tom is writing to your papa this very minute, that we will take you home with us to New York."

"To New York!" said the little girl, with her eyes very wide open; "then, — shall we not see Palemke, and the baby?"

STATUE AT COPAN.

"You will see the baby when she is a little older, I dare say," said Bessie; "and as for Palemke, it will not make a great deal of difference if it is a little older before you see it."

"That's so," said the little girl, who was picking up, no one knew where, several Yankee expressions, and she went to sleep well contented.

"We may as well settle upon that," Tom had remarked, as he dipped his pen into the ink. "I must write something by this mail, and this will afford a basis of operations for Mr. Johnstone."

"Perhaps it is as well, but Mrs J. will be terribly excited," said Bessie. "What do you think, aunt Dut?"

Miss Augusta had been obliged to give up the defence of her early friend, in these discussions, for she was forced to admit that the discipline of life had not developed a mind with originally amiable, but not forcible qualities.

CHAPTER XXX.

THE NATIONAL MUSEUM.

THE large rooms and corridors of the Museum of Antiquities run round a spacious patio planted with tall palm-trees, laid out with walks and flower beds, upon which are set some of the largest specimens left of Aztec stone-work. The position of these is changed from time to time. When the Horners were there the central piece was the great Sacrificial stone of the Mexicans, upon which they sacrificed human victims. It is covered with carvings representing warlike contests, to explain which theories have been formed by those who have studied them. The children had already so horrible an idea of the blood-thirsty nature of the sacrifices perpetrated upon the stone, that they hurried past it with a shudder, and the grown-up people did not care to detain them.

Chac-mool, who may be seen in the picture sunning himself in the patio, is now tucked away in the long room at the back of the court. This room was in process of re-arrangement, and alguazils sternly forbade an entrance, but Miss Lejeune, holding Helena by the hand, pushed in amid trestles and ladders, and falling plaster, so that they might look at the effigy of the Tiger King from Chichen-Itza.

Meanwhile, Jack, escorted by Tom, was staring at the state-coach of Maximilian, in another room leading from the court, but Bessie refused to look at anything later than Montezuma, and she and the Marches were on their way up-stairs when the others hurried to join them.

They found later, from the catalogue, that the Palemke tablet

COURT OF THE NATIONAL MUSEUM.

which they especially wished to see, was below, and did not fail to look at it when they came back.

As they were all, by this time, curious about the ancient civilization of the Aztecs, they found the vases, urns, jugs displayed in the different cases, most interesting, noting that the simple grace of form the Indians now give to their pottery is a direct inheritance from their ancestors.

Grotesque designs were abundant, and efforts at representing faces and figures made with great directness.

The children wanted to find out the story of all the paintings, which, tattered and stained, are stretched upon the walls. These paintings were the books of the early Mexicans; they had no alphabet, but, instead of letters, used pictured signs which answered just as well. The figures seem grotesque and mis-shapen, but they were full of meaning; colors as well as forms had their separate significance. The art of writing and reading these pictures was taught by priests, and handed down from one generation to another.

Among the first ambassadors sent to meet Cortés by Montezuma were painters, who rapidly took notes as a modern reporter might, to transmit to their monarch an account of the strange arrival. They faithfully depicted every detail of costume, arms, ships, horses, — these fearful animals they had no previous practice in drawing; and thus, on their return to their court, the sovereign could judge for himself the importance of the invasion, as well as if he had received an extra edition of his morning paper.

Unfortunately the Spaniards destroyed quantities of these picture-writings, which might have told us all the story of the wanderings of the early tribes, as well as the civilization of the Mexican races.

At the museum is a plaster cast of the famous Aztec calendar, which can be there studied to better advantage than the genuine stone one now built into the side of the cathedral. The real one is considered the property of the Museum, but it forms a part of the stone-work of the Cathedral.

It is said to have been brought from a long way off by the Aztecs to Tenochtitlan, their city which stood on the site of the present city of Mexico, in 1512. As it was borne over the causeway leading from the main land to the island city, its weight broke down the floating bridge on which it was loaded, and it fell into the lake. The High Priest and many of his assistants were drowned. It was raised with great labor and borne to the temple of the God of War, with celebrations and awful human sacrifices. This was not many years before the Spaniards destroyed all the temples. They buried this great stone, and many of the idols in the marshes surrounding the lake, where they remained unsuspected and forgotten. In 1790 it was found in the earth beneath the Plaza Mayor, near to the Cathedral then in process of construction, and the Viceroy consented to its being set into the base of one of the towers.

It bears the signs of the Zodiac as conceived by the Mexicans, and served as a calendar for their year, which had three hundred and sixty-five days, like ours, but was divided into eighteen months of twenty days each, and these months into four weeks of only five days each. The days had funny names, such as "Rabbit," "Monkey," "Small bird," etc.

The Aztecs moved large masses of stone by means of a long file of men dragging them with ropes over great wooden rollers, much as the Egyptians moved stones for their pyramids.

The rooms of the museum contain many other things of historical import, — the portraits of all the Spanish viceroys, sixty-two in all, of which the only one the children cared to look at was Mendoza, the good founder of Morelia. A portrait of Cortés detained them a long time, while they cast but a passing glance at the silver, or plated, table service of Maximilian, displayed in a great glass-case.

Bessie collected all the party before a little modern oil-painting very prettily executed of a place she much wished to visit, but which they had to give up for this time. It was the "Bath of Nezahualcoyotl" at Tezcoco, and represented a great porphyry rock high up in the air hollowed out like a bird's-nest. A winding path led to it, and revealed in the distance a wide-stretching belt of bird's-eye view of the lake of Tezcoco, the valley, and the city in the distance. Bessie told the children to look hard at the picture, and that she would tell them about the place later. And then they all walked home, very tired, for there is nothing so tiring as looking, with intelligence, all through a museum of curiosities. The eyes refuse to see anything, after a time, but rows of glass-cases, the brain stops taking in any information, and the legs become so weary that standing up appears an impossibility.

"Let us get away from here immediately," said Miss Lejeune, "I feel as if I should drop."

"Did you see those two people sitting on a bench;" asked Bessie, as they went down stairs, "I believe they were there from sheer inability to go away. I think they will sit there forever and be gradually turned to stone. That is exactly the way I feel after I have been long in the museum; as if all the things in my head had been moved out and set up in cases with labels on."

"So do I," said Tom, "only the attack comes on sooner with me. Children, run, for fear you should be turned into Aztec remains, and have numbers pinned on in front."

The children were over willing to run, and skipped happily down the stairs and out into the street.

"I am glad that is accomplished," sighed Miss Lejeune, as she opened her parasol; "but if we were here longer we would go often. It would be nice to sit in that cool corridor looking down upon the palm-trees in the court."

Mr. March laughed. "That," he said, "is what we thought the first time we came, but we have not been very often. There are so many churches to see, and so many expeditions in cars outside the city, and then," —

"And then," interrupted his wife, "it is so good to stay at home and not go anywhere."

"That is what I like," promptly said Miss Lejeune. "It is the best part of travelling."

Nezahualcoyotl was the greatest of the Chichimec kings, whose capital was Tezcoco. He formed a code of laws which were wise and just, opened schools and colleges, built palaces and gardens and many works of public utility. He reigned from 1431 to 1472, and left behind him a great name.

The picture represented his favorite home at Tezcotziuco, on a conical hill not far from the capital. It was laid out in terraces or hanging gardens, and on the summit was a reservoir brought for several miles over hill and valley from which the water fell in numerous channels and cascades throughout the gardens to keep the flowers fresh. The rocks were carved with figures representing the years of his reign and his great achievements.

Here the great King of the Chichimec dynasty flourished, and ruled with dignity and wisdom; one hundred years afterwards, his descendant, Ixtlilxochitl, the fourteenth and last monarch of his race, was an ardent and faithful ally of the Spanish invaders from their first appearance in the country. Without his aid, it would have gone hard with Cortés upon his second attack of the city of Mexico; for it was to his capital city, Tezcoco, that Cortés returned, only a few months after his sad flight, with a new army reinforced by Indian allies, with eighty-six horse, and plenty of ammunition.

Tezcoco was the best possible position for him to take. As its territories bordered on those of the Tlascalans, Cortés could keep up intercourse with the country of those valuable allies, and it was near enough to Mexico for him to watch that capital.

A palace was assigned to him, and the young king showed himself anxious to do everything to forward his plans.

Cortés had with him a number of brigantines, vessels made in

NEZAHUALCOYOTL.

Tlascala and brought in parts all ready to be put together when they reached the water. Tezcoco was at some distance from the lake, so a canal was dug by Indians from the gardens of Nezahualcoyotl to receive the vessels when they were launched, so that they could float to the entrance of the lake.

In short, Ixtlilxochitl did everything to help the subjugation of Mexico. He was later baptized as a Christian under the name of Ferdinand, and accompanied Cortés on several of his later expeditions.

CHAPTER XXXI.

THE END OF THE CONQUEST.

THE canal from Tezcoco to the lake was finished after having employed eight thousand men for two months. It was a work of great labor. The brigantines were launched upon it with grand ceremonies and carried down to the lake. At a signal given by the firing of a cannon, the vessels entered the canal one after another, and reached the lake in good order, with the royal ensign of Castile floating from their masts, and martial music sounding.

Cortés then mustered his forces, which made a better show than at any time before. He divided them into three separate camps, which he put at the three ends of the principal causeways, thus, with the vessels on the lake, completely surrounding the city. The first step was to cut off the pipes of the royal aqueduct leading from Chapultepec. This was not accomplished without a battle, for the Indians were well aware of the importance of protecting their supply of water; but the Spaniards succeeded in destroying a part of it, so that no water reached the capital through this channel during the siege.

It was in the latter part of May that the attack was fairly begun, and not until August 13 was the determined spirit of the besieged city broken. Their condition was terrible; starvation and disease aided their enemies, but the resolution of the Mexicans was firm till the last.

Cuauhtemoc (Guatemozin) did prodigies of valor, and heartily refused every proposition of Cortés for accommodation. At the last, he embarked with his family in one of the *piraguas*, small boats, upon the lake, vainly hoping to escape the vigilance of the brigantines which were close at hand. His little boat was pursued and overtaken, he was captured and brought into the presence of the Spanish commander. Cuauhtemoc was easily distinguished from his attendant nobles. His head was large, his complexion fairer than common with his race, his whole bearing calm and regal. He said, "I have done all I could to defend myself and my people, now, deal with me, Malinche, as you list."

Cortés treated him with great courtesy, and sent for his wife. She was the youngest daughter of Montezuma, and is said to have been very beautiful. Cortés received her kindly, and invited his royal captives to partake of refreshment which, no doubt, they sorely needed. It was the hour of vespers when the Mexican monarch surrendered, and the siege was over.

The next day the Mexicans were allowed to leave the city, and for three days they moved off along the causeways, many thousand men, beside women and children who had survived the contest, pestilence and famine. Cortés was glad to have them go, in order to cleanse and purify the place, which was in a terrible condition.

The king, Cuauhtemoc, was retained. At first he was treated with great consideration, but afterwards he was put to the torture by the cruel Spaniards, to make him reveal to them where the royal treasures were concealed. They were much disappointed to find but little booty in the conquered city, and they were convinced that there were jewels and gold hidden somewhere. All that could be wrung from the suffering monarch was that much gold had been thrown into the water. He was released finally, and lived in captivity several years longer. When Cortés made the expedition to Honduras, at the time that he passed by Palemke without knowing it, the Aztec king accompanied him. On the way, a rumor came to the ears of Cortés that his native prisoners were conspiring against him, and the unfortunate princes, Cuauhtemoc among them, were hung, without delay, on the high branches of a great tree upon the road.

Thus perished on the twenty-sixth of February, 1525, this young and brave monarch, the last of the Aztecs, for with him terminated the monarchy founded by his ancestors in 1376.

Meanwhile Cortés set about rebuilding the capital, and founding the city which is now standing. In less than four years, a new city had risen upon the ruins of the old. He applied himself to settling the rest of the country, and encouraging the immigration of new comers. The *conquistadores* settled wherever they liked. The silver mines which have since been so great a source of wealth, had already begun to be known, to realize in part the dream of the first explorers, but their real riches came from the soil, which Cortés wisely caused to be cultivated and developed.

"And so," said Bessie, "that is about the end of the conquest of Mexico. All the great Aztecs were dead, and the population settled down gradually, accepting the Christian religion which was taught them zealously by the priests, who were in general kind and good people. The first viceroys, like Mendoza, did the best they could for them, and so in time the natives came to be the simple, gentle, superstitious people we see here, contented with their lot, keeping up their festivals, with flowers and dances much the same as they were in old times, only that the worship of the gentle Virgin is substituted for that of their fearful old war-gods, and human sacrifices are entirely done away with.

" And what became of Cortés?" asked Jack.

"And what became of Doña Marina?" squeaked Helena.

"Oh! I must tell you about Marina," said Bessie. "I am glad you have not forgotten her, Helena.

"When Cortés went to Honduras, she was with him, and they passed through her native country. Who should turn up there but her horrid old mother, who had sold her, you know, to some traders when she was a little girl. She came to a conference ordered by Cortés with the caciques of the neighborhood, and she had her son with her, and as soon as they appeared, every one was struck with the likeness between this son and Marina; and Marina recognized her mother and ran up to her. The old lady was pretty well frightened, but her daughter was very good to her, and gave her some pretty ornaments she was wearing, telling her that everything had turned out for the best, as she much preferred being a Christian. So she bade her mother good-by, and went away, and that was the last ever heard of her unnatural relatives. On that same expedition Marina was married to a Castilian knight, named Don Juan Xamarillo. Estates were assigned to her in her native provinces, and there she probably passed the rest of her life.

"She has always been held in grateful remembrance for her usefulness to the Spaniards. Her Indian name was Malinche, by which she is commemorated in many native ballads, and her spirit is said to hover about the capital she helped to win.

"As for Cortés, he was apppointed Governor of New Spain, by Charles the Fifth, and captain-general as well. He devoted himself to the interests of his hardly-earned realm for a few years, but was obliged to go to Spain in 1528, to answer accusations brought against him by people who were jealous of his power. He was received at court with great honor, and made the marquis of a province consisting of lands given to him by Montezuma. The government of the country was taken from him, but he retained the highest military rank. He married a lovely bride, much younger than himself, — a Spanish lady of noble birth. One of his presents to her consisted of five wonderful emeralds cut by the Aztecs into fanciful shapes, — flowers, fishes and birds. It is said that the Queen of Spain would have liked these pretty toys for herself, and that she was so much offended with Cortés for not giving them to her instead of to his bride, that she lost her interest in him, and even exerted her influence against him.

However this may be, he wearied of the idle luxury of the court and returned to Mexico, where he built a great palace upon his estates and lived quietly.

"In 1540, he returned to Spain, having grown dissatisfied with the course of the viceroy, Mendoza. He was honorably received at court, but treated with indifference. He was no longer the hero of the hour. His demands were disregarded, and after hanging round for some time, waiting for notice in a humiliating position, he resolved to go back to Mexico.

"He had gone no farther than Seville, when he was attacked by illness, and there, in a neighboring village he died, on the second of December, 1547, without again seeing the land of his labors and triumphs. He was sixty-two, not an old man, but his life had been filled with adventure and varying fortune enough for several lives of common men.

"He was buried with great honor in Seville, and, could he have been present at his own funeral, would have been comforted by its splendor for the indifference with which his last years had been passed over. His body was removed later to Tezcoco, in New Spain, and in fact the restless career of his life was prolonged after the spirit had left the body, for twice afterwards was its repose disturbed, that it might be carried with pomp and ceremony from one sepulchre to another."

In 1823, the patriot mob of the capital in their zeal against the old Spanish rule, were prepared to break open the tomb of Cortés, and scatter his ashes to the wind. Friends of the family secretly entered the vault and removed them.

There are no longer living any direct male descendants of Fernando Cortés. The title and estates, in the fourth generation, came to an heiress, who married a descendant of Gonsalvo de Cordova, and thus her children and grandchildren could boast a descent from two illustrious warriors, the Gran Capitan, and the Conquistador

CHAPTER XXXII.

LAST DAYS IN THE CAPITAL.

THE Marches, with Tom and Bessie, came into the corner room one day, where they found Miss Lejeune over her letters. She looked up over her spectacles,— a recent but imperative innovation,— and said briefly,

"Where are the children?"

"With Jules, who is setting the private table for a grand déjeûner."

"So much the better; what do you think has happened?"

They all recognized the large blue paper and strongly marked handwriting of Mr. Johnstone.

"He has discovered the key to the hieroglyphics," suggested one.

"The baby has fallen down-stairs," said another.

"Mrs. Johnstone has eloped," proposed Tom.

"None of those things, but equally serious," said Miss Lejeune. "Minton has struck. She cannot get along with the Mayan servant, she finds *chile* and *pulque* do not agree with her, and, as Mrs. Johnstone is pretty well, and has taken to going off on expeditions of two or three days with her husband, Minton cannot stand being left all alone with the natives."

"I do not much wonder," said Bessie; "but what next?"

"That is what I am reserving, till your minds are prepared for it," said Miss Lejeune. "Minton has already taken a return steamer for New York *via* Havana," —

"What's to become of the baby!" they all cried.

"The baby is with her," she continued, "and —"

"Mrs. Johnstone is with the baby!" shrieked Tom.

"Right you are, Thomas," assented Miss Lejeune, with an air of complete enjoyment, caused entirely by the satisfaction of announcing that singular news, without any present thought of the consequences, or of the bearings upon their own movements.

"Gone," said Bessie, as a statement, not a question. "Actually sailed. They must be nearly at New York by this time."

Miss Lejeune put down the letter, hid her face in her handkerchief and laughed, in a sort of tearful way. The rest looked blank, were silent, slowly taking hold of the situation.

"How futile!" remarked Bessie, at last. It was a brief comment upon the trouble and fuss which had attended the departure of the Johnstones. Miss Lejeune's willing sacrifice of her quiet life at home to accompany her friend, the expense of the expedition, the superfluous trip to and from Mexico, the outfit, the house at Merida, and lastly, the prolonged separation between these parents and their two elder children, were all made useless by the weak desertion of her post, by Mrs. Johnstone, leaving her husband to settle everything.

"What does he say?" said Tom.

"Well, he says, among other things, that it is very sudden," said Miss Lejeune, wiping her eyes; "he says he shall be very grateful if *we* will hit upon some plan."

"The only plan," said Tom, thrusting his hands into his pockets, and walking up and down, "is for us to find the orphan asylum for Aztecs, and put the two children there this afternoon."

Bessie made a sign to Tom not to go on in this vein. She saw that Miss Lejeune was a good deal upset by the news, feeling, as she often had through the expedition, that she had brought the Johnstones upon the rest, and that everything uncomfortable in the trip was therefore her fault.

"The only plan," said Bessie serenely, "is for us to take the children home with us, and hand them over to their mother. She will

INTERIOR OF THE CATHEDRAL OF MEXICO.

probably pause in her wild flight when she arrives in New York."

"Poor Marianne," said Augusta, her eyes again filling with tears.

"Don't fret about her, Dut," said Tom, now coming to sit down by her, "she will be all right as soon as she is at home; we can write her at once that we will bring the children, and there is nothing to prevent our going very soon. I have had about enough of this."

"Oh! there is another thing, I forgot," said Miss Augusta, brightening, "an invitation to Miraflores."

"To Miraflores, delightful!" cried Mr. March, who, with his wife, had been a silent observer of the discussion up to this point.

"Is it not kind of the Robsons?" said Miss Lejeune. "It would be lovely to go, but," —

"The children!" said Bessie with solemnity; and then there was a pause.

"We will take care of the children," exclaimed Mr. March. "Katharine, my dear, you have long been intending to adopt four or five orphans; this is precisely your opportunity."

"Why, certainly," replied Mrs. March, "only we have not much room, — still it can be arranged."

"We will go somewhere," said her husband. "I will tell you; when you three start for Miraflores, we will go on the same train to Amecameca, which we have been so long planning for. The hotel there is vile, I am told, but that is no matter. Hullo! Jack," he added, as that young gentleman entered the room, "do not you want to go to Amecameca with us?"

"Yes, I do," replied the boy, "what is Amecameca?"

And thus it was decided. A day was fixed for leaving the city, the invitation to Miraflores was gratefully, and with enthusiasm accepted, and then all minds were turned to seeing and doing last things; for it seemed best to give up finally the rooms at the Café Anglais on leaving, sending heavy luggage to the station, and merely crossing the town, or stopping a few hours, before taking the Mexican Central train for the great departure, when the Miraflores visit was over.

The Marches were most excellent. They took the children in hand at once, carrying them to see places in the capital, which the Horners never knew anything about, like the Plaza of San Domingo, with the church on one side, containing some beautiful gilt wood-work. They saw the interior of the Cathedral, which Miss Lejeune did not go near, and went into many churches, and out-of-the-way picturesque places. They made an expedition which the others should not have neglected, to Guadalupe, where, in the Cathedral, hangs a famous picture of the Virgin, with a wonderful tradition attached to it.

The Virgin Mary appeared to an Indian several times, and told him that she wanted a temple built upon the place. The Indian reported the apparition to the bishop of Mexico, but he would not believe anything about it; then the vision told him to gather flowers and take them to the bishop, to convince him. And lo! the bare, dry mountain-side was suddenly all covered with flowers, which the amazed Indian gathered until he had filled his *tilma* or cloak. He ran with them to the bishop and shook them out upon the floor before him, when all of a sudden the bishop fell upon his knees before the outspread cloak, for there, on the inside of it, where the flowers had touched the poor garment, was a glowing picture of the Blessed Virgin herself! The church was built after that, and named after Our Lady of Guadalupe.

It was the picture of the Virgin of Guadalupe which Hidalgo's little army bore on the night of the first uprising. The very banner is deposited in the chapel at Guadalupe.

This story of the supernatural appearance of the Virgin to an Indian, had a powerful effect in converting the Aztecs, used to superstitions and signs, who felt that such a miracle shared by one of their own race connected them all with Christians; the result was the conversion of many of them; Our Lady of Guadalupe is a favorite object of worship all over Mexico, where the Mother of God, as she is called, is regarded with intense love and devotion. For the Saviour, the feelings of the *peones* may be composed of respectful pity, and distant adoration, but to the Virgin they give their hearts, and seem to reverence her as a splendid queen, who looks with pity and compassion upon their sufferings, because she herself has suffered.

From the little chapel on the hill there is a fine view of the valley of Mexico. In front of it is a strange monument carved out of stone, in the form of a mast and sails, the offering of a sailor who was protected in a storm at sea, by the watchfulness of Our Lady of Guadalupe.

These last days were so crowded and hurried that the party broke up into little groups of two or three, arranging their time carefully in the early morning, and perhaps not meeting all together until the late dinner at night, when they recited their different adventures.

The Marches were active and helpful, always ready to suggest occupations for the children, to find trains on time-tables, and above all to join in talking over the events of the day.

There is always a joyous, fatiguing sort of hurry about the last days in the last city of a foreign tour. In this case there seemed no exact reason for it, except as the inevitable attribute of a final departure. The confusion can be easily accounted for in Paris or London, when a whole family is starting off for America, by the feeling, which is still a common one, that they may never come back. Last glimpses of monuments, one last flight through the Louvre, one final search over the counters of the Bon Marché, are crowded into a few days. There were not so many imperative matters on hand in the city of Mexico, especially as all the party were fully persuaded they should come back another year, yet everyone was possessed by the demon who wishes to crowd every moment with a bit of sight-seeing or shopping. Perhaps Miss Lejeune was unconsciously actuated by a sense that her travelling days were over, and that this would be the last time she would be implicated into the confusion of final preparations.

Her own last expedition was alone, through the arcades of the Municipal Palace, where she bought three more scrapes and three more rebozos.

"Why, aunt Dut!" cried Bessie, "you are insatiable; how many have you got?"

"This makes only eleven scrapes in all," she said.

MUNICIPAL PALACE.

CHAPTER XXXIII.

MIRAFLORES.

SO, early one morning, they found themselves at the station of the Morelos railroad, all bound in the same direction as far as La Compañia, where Miss Lejeune, with Tom and Bessie, branched off for Miraflores, while the Marches conveyed Jack and Helena further on to Amecameca.

Morelos is one of the States of Mexico, and the railroad which bears its name passes through the State on its way to Acapulco, on the Pacific Ocean. It has crept as far as Cuautla, some fifty miles from the capital, a lovely city which the Marches had been to several times, and which they were always praising for its lovely climate, more tropical than that of Mexico, luxuriant verdure, and profuse flowers.

"We should insist on your going to Cuautla," said Mrs. March, "if it were a month or two earlier; but now it would be altogether unsafe on account of malaria, and altogether too warm for enjoyment. In the early winter Cuautla is perfect."

The Morelos railway is not well managed at present, — unlike the National, which the Horners knew to be prompt and punctual to a minute, and the Mexican Central which they were soon to prove equally so. Here was tedious delay before the train left the city, and at every station long waits which seemed endless, in spite of the fun to be had buying tortillas and tomales, and packages of figs.

It was a ride of several hours, unnecessarily long, before the two parties separated. Jack and Helena went on with Mr. and

Mrs. March to Amecameca, a little village at the foot of Popocatepetl, from which the ascent of that mountain is best made. Our party had no such ambition, although it is for this purpose only that tourists generally seek the place, where there is but a wretched little hotel; but the views of both the great volcanoes, Popocatepetl and Istaccinuatl, is superb, and well worth undergoing an uncomfortable night. The mountains appear close at hand, as Mt. Blanc and the rest do at Chamouni.

At last the children had a good chance to see the famous peaks they had learned by heart in their geographies. Popocatepetl is seventeen thousand seven hundred and twenty feet above sea level,— nearly half a mile higher than Mt. Blanc, and its companion is but little less. Istac$c_i$huatl, which should be emphasized at ci, means the "White Woman," and the outline is not unlike a female form stretched out as if upon a bier, and covered with a shroud;

LUXURIANT VERDURE.

for the snow never leaves the summit, but lies forever like a mantle on its undulating lines, bringing them out sharp and clear against the sky.

Meanwhile Miss Lejeune, with Bessie and Tom, were enjoying the most delightful days of their Mexican trip; days which were to be counted among the most delightful of their lives. They went by tram-car to Miraflores, the home of an English family, whose kindly, hospitable hearts had been opened to them by the key of a letter from some mutual friends very dear to both parties. And here for two days they enjoyed real hospitality in the most charming country seat in the most beautiful situation. The long, low house was overhung with vines, and banked with

ANCIENT TEMPLE.

geraniums and other bright flowers. An ample garden, so long established that it was shaded by large trees, yet full of sunshine, was a paradise of roses, in luxuriant blossom. These roses grew on standards sometimes five or six feet high, and were of every imaginable kind, like the most precious of hothouse varieties. There were white roses, yellow roses, flame-colored ones; deep crimson, warm rose-color, and the palest pink; roses as large as your open hand, and crowded with petals, single dogroses, and old-fashioned "cinnamon roses." They grew in such profusion, that their faded petals fell in heaps unheeded, and swept away by the tidy gardener, while the neglected blossoms he cut off would have made the fortune of a florist. Everybody could have all he could possibly desire. The difficulty was to choose. Each new blossom seemed more lovely than the rest, and when a handful was gathered, every separate one seemed the most worthy of praise.

Bessie and Miss Lejeune were wild about the roses. They wanted to be painting them all the time. But the roses were not all. Heliotrope was trained up the side of the house, and looked in at the window of their large comfortable room, — on the ground-floor, as were all the rooms, full of fragrant blossoms. The high wall running round the garden, and shutting in this fairy enclosure was massed with morning-glories of intense blue. Bignonia hung from every angle, and pansies, sweet-peas, with countless other flowers, bloomed in the beds bordered by the rose-trees.

It was an enchanted spot. Water trickled from fountains among the walks, and kept the place always fresh. There were seats under the trees, where one might look out upon the sunny wealth of blossoms, and try to decide which rose to gather next.

When they had begun to be the least bit accustomed to the lovely spot, and could bear to restrain themselves from exclaiming, "How enchanting!" more than once in five minutes, some one said, "Go and bring the key to the *Alfalfa* gate," and they were led to a thick door in the high wall. All around them was shade, seclusion, and the perfume of roses. The gate was thrown open, and a broad, wide-reaching view spread before and below them, of sunny fields glowing green with rich alfalfa (clover) stretching far, far away, and the horizon bounded by the grand forms of the two volcanoes, Istaccihuatl and Popocatepetl, glowing in the light of the sunset which was fast approaching.

It was a wonderful view; beyond exclamations of approval, or words to describe it. Steps led down to a broad gravel walk, lined with flower-beds, leading around the outer enclosure of these grounds, with glimpses of the distance between trees; it was all very pretty, but our travellers returned with rapture to the view from the Alfalfa gate.

To describe this visit in detail would be to trespass upon the hospitality which made it perfect. The guests who enjoyed it will look back upon it rather as a dream than as a possible reality, — as brief, as bright, as perfect dreams ought to be.

It had this element of unreality the more, that as soon as it was over, our party was plunged into extreme agitation and hurry, by the receipt of a telegram which awaited them on their return to the city. It said:

Mrs. Johnstone here, — very ill; you must bring children immediately.
CLARENCE HERVEY.

Luckily the children did not see the message, for Tom tore it open in the office, before joining the party. He took Miss Lejeune aside to show it to her, and they decided, upon consultation, not to alarm Jack and Helena at present.

Their rooms at the Café Anglais had been given up, but they had arranged to have one more dinner there before driving to the Mexican Central Station, for the evening train. A merry last meeting had been planned, and the Marches only went to their rooms to re-fit before presenting themselves for the feast. Jules and the *chef* had outdone themselves to make the *menu* worthy of so serious an occasion.

"Let us keep on so with it," said Miss Lejeune. "I will tell Bessie, and you can tell the Marches, but the children need not know. I suppose we had better—"

"Better give up Santa Fé, and Colorado City, and stopping in Chicago," finished Tom promptly. "Of course,—and, after all, I do not care much about it this time."

"Nor I, Tom,—Tom, I long to get home!" exclaimed Miss Lejeune, and strangely enough for her, she burst into tears.

They were sitting in a mysterious little room at the top of the round winding-stair leading from the restaurant of the Café Anglais. It was but a parenthesis between two corridors,—the outer one and the gallery of the patio,—but it was carpeted and curtained, and contained cosey furniture and a commodious desk, where the proprietor made out the bills, and issued those mandates which so admirably regulated his hotel.

"This is no place for a scene, my dear," she hastened to say, recovering herself at once, and rising from the low chair upon which she had dropped.

"Let me order a room for you. I dare say your own is vacant," cried Tom.

"No, no; I am all right, only a little tired,—and,—poor Mari anne !" she sobbed, for she had broken down again.

Tom knelt down by her and put his arm round her, and soothed her in the most tender way.

"Poor dear aunt Dut, you are too tired, and too worried to go on; we will not think of it until to-morrow."

But this Miss Lejeune would not listen to. She mastered her emotion, and was soon ready to join the rest, and with more exertion than was usual to her of late, kept the little party merry, if not really joyous, through the dinner.

They sat for the last time around their little table in one of the small side rooms of the Café Anglais. It was just big enough to hold them, with a little crowding, and very snug, lighted from above. Jules and the proprietor vied with each other in their parting attentions; the special dishes they liked had been prepared for them.

Artichokes, green peas and strawberries were a part of the dinner, — luxuries they did not hope to see for a long time.

The children were in fine spirits, little suspecting the anxiety of the rest about their mother, and ready for the new adventure of a whole week in a sleeping car.

"So you will go right through," said Mr. March to Tom, as they were waiting for the bill in the office.

"Yes," said Tom, "the ladies are resolved to try it. It will be fatiguing for them, I fear."

"Seven days and seven nights," said Mr. March, "yes, that is pretty long. Still, we have found it about as comfortable as breaking the journey. You are not very much rested by one night at a hotel, and you are too tired for sight-seeing. But you will miss Colorado Springs."

"It cannot be helped," replied Tom, "and, on the whole, I am glad for Miss Lejeune. Bessie and I both think she seems tired. The whole Johnstone business has worried her, and she will be glad to be at home."

CHAPTER XXXIV.

DEPARTURE.

IT was nearly eight o'clock in the evening, and all the party were assembled in the station of the Mexican Central Railroad, vast and commodious, brilliantly lighted with electricity. Miss Lejeune and Bessie entered the car with fear and trembling, for this was the first experience of either of them of a long journey in sleepers. Of course they had been from Boston to New York, or Washington, with one night of it, but now they were in for seven days and seven nights of consecutive travel,

Each in her narrow cell forever laid,

as Bessie misquoted.

But it was the peculiarity of each of them to be seized with an attack of good spirits the minute they entered any form of travelling conveyance; a gayety which was well justified in the present case, for nothing can be more inviting and attractive than a palace-car, all swept and garnished, and brightly lighted, for a fresh start on a long journey. The long vista of the empty car shining with brass and polished wood, the warm cushions of the plush-covered seats, and the soft lights of suspended lamps, suggested luxury and comfort, and after the shabby, crowded cars of the Morelos railway they had so lately left, their new quarters seemed spacious. There was room enough over their heads and under their feet for all their bags and straps.

"This is really a palace," cried Bessie, and she danced down the long narrow passage-way covered with a strip of soft carpet. Her progress was somewhat impeded by the stiff row of spittoons placed at regular distances, which is an inevitable part of the furniture of these cars; but she gave them little kicks as she passed. "I hope we shall have it all to ourselves," she cried; "there can't be many people going all the way to New York."

They had secured the stateroom at the end of the car, and Miss Lejeune was to occupy this with Helena, while Bessie had

INTERIOR OF CAR.

the lower berth of a compartment close to the stateroom, and Tom and Jack the whole section opposite her, with upper and lower berth; so they were all grouped together, and felt as if they formed a little colony for mutual protection. They were only able to engage the stateroom and adjacent section as far as El

Paso, where they would have to change cars, but they hoped to make the same arrangement all through.

It was very convenient for the moment to poke all their impediments into the stateroom; for a little group of friends began at once to assemble, and these they received in the seats belonging to Bessie's section and the one opposite. The Marches were there, of course, and kind Mrs. Morgan had sent by some of her family a basket of provisions against the terrors of the restaurants they were to encounter on the journey. While they were all laughing and talking, who should come in but Mr. Pastor. They had not seen him since they parted at Morelia. Wonderful to relate, he had come, not to bid them good-by, but because he was going too! He had received leave of absence for six weeks, and coming to Mexico, hastened at once to the Café Anglais to see the Horners and find out their plans. They were off already for Miraflores, but he learned easily what day was fixed for their departure, and at once decided upon it for his own.

"What an agreeable surprise!" said Miss Lejeune. "Our party always needs one more, and you are just the addition we require."

Mr. Pastor bowed. "The privilege is all on my side," he replied; "there is all the difference in the world between a solitary jaunt over these long stretches, and a lively journey with such companions."

These interchanges of mutual compliment filled up the time. Several gentlemen had come with Mr. Pastor to see him off. These were introduced all round, though nobody remembered their names for a moment, or even how they looked. Jules was still lingering, bustling about, and arranging little matters for their greater convenience. Almost at the last, a messenger brought an immense fresh bouquet of roses from the wonderful garden at Miraflores.

Time was up, the final whistle shrieked. The car was cleared, and slowly rolled out of the station. The last they saw of Mexico was Mr. March, standing on the platform with his hat raised, in the full white light of the electric lamps. "Hasta luego!" was their last cry, — and then with a little sigh of regret at leaving so many kind friends, and a country, which in so short a time they had learned to love so much, they all set about making ready for the night.

The excitement of the first impression was over. Bessie began already to feel a cold chill of doubt creeping over her, as to the perfect bliss of her situation. The car was rumbling along with a dull, steady sound, swaying a little from side to side. A few travellers scattered along through the car, took away the feeling that her party had it all to themselves. The light seemed less brilliant and more as if you could not read by it, and when she began to gather her things about her, in spite of the small compass into which she flattered herself she had pressed them, she found they had filled up pretty much all the space she had to live in.

The first thing was to get Helena to bed, and while Tom and Mr. Pastor went off to smoke, Bessie summoned the porter to make up their berths.

The porter, in a sleeper, is a very important personage, and it is highly desirable to get on the right side of him at once. He is black, and while the train is in the station, gorgeous in the undress uniform of the railroad, with a gilt band to his cap. When he reappears after the car has started, he is transformed. In a white jacket and flat white cap, he glides along the passages like a dark gnome, transforming seats to beds with a strange magic, which gives a sense of supernatural power belonging to him.

Helena sat, in awe, by Bessie's side, while the porter made the beds in the stateroom. They were in the outer car, but could look through the little door and see him at it. First he let down the slanting ceiling of the car with a bang, and Helena perceived that the space behind it was a great box full of pillows and blankets and beds. He took more pillows out of the boxes under the seats below, and by a few dexterous turns of his hand, converted the space where the seats were into a broad flat bed, while the ceiling he had let down made a second bed above. Then he went away, to a little tall, narrow cupboard he had, and brought out a pile of clean sheets. In a twinkling he had made the upper berth, poking and patting it in a series of leaps from below; soon the lower bed was ready also. Both were covered with dark striped blankets, and had plump pillows in fresh white pillow-cases at the heads. The window shades were pulled down and fastened close; and finally heavy curtains were hung before the berths, falling from the roof to the floor, and hiding both beds with their heavy folds. It was very wonderful, Helena thought, and she looked along the car with amazement, at all the slanting-places now full of pillows, and mattresses, and blankets, soon to be spread out for beds. She was quickly undressed, and scrambled up into her berth as she had early learned to do on the steamer, and in less than a minute she was sound asleep, the steady rumbling of the wheels lending itself to her dreams.

"I hate to leave you out here, Bessie," said Miss Lejeune as she prepared to shut herself into the stateroom.

"Don't think of it," said Bessie. "I am all right; here is Jack, you see, and I shall soon be safe in my berth. We are so tired, there is no danger of my not sleeping, I fancy."

"Good-night, then!"

"Good-night!"

Gradually, as Bessie and Jack sat in a vacant place, they saw the car transformed into a long double row of berths, which, one by one, unfolded themselves and filled the place, till nothing was to be seen but a narrow vista of waving curtains. Then she and Jack disappeared each behind his own.

For this night only, Bessie enjoyed the whole section. The lower berth alone was hers by right; for the cost of a whole section is just double, and on so long a journey, it seemed extravagant to pay for it. By an amiable forgetfulness on the part of the porter, the upper berth was left closed that night, in the slanting position it occupies in the daytime; but this is against all rules, and it never happened again. Bessie was most grateful for the accident, for, at the best, her quarters seemed but narrow, and she could not imagine how to breathe with the top down.

In the first place, it was hot, very hot. There was a thick blanket tucked down tightly all round, and stuffy closed curtains before her berth kept out whatever little air there was, as the ventilators were almost all closed. Her head seemed to her to be directly on the wheels, without any intervention of pillow, bed, or flooring, so that her ear was forced to listen to their every creak and turn. The lights were not put out till long after she had turned in, and as she was among the first to retire, she had to hear the last words of every one else in the car, and to watch through a crack in the curtain, all their preliminary preparations for the night. She felt herself growing more and more wide awake, and had to put a strong force upon herself not to become nervous and restless. By and by Tom came back, having left Mr. Pastor at the other end of the car, where his berth was.

"Tom," said Bessie softly, "this is dreadful!"

"What's the matter? are you not all right?"

"I am nearly roasted," she replied, "and the car makes a terrible noise, and I am sure that man in the top berth next you is going to snore."

"Has he begun?" asked Tom, laughing.

"No; he has not gone to bed yet. He is sitting out there by the door, but he is just built for it."

"I will go and push him off the platform, if you like," said Tom, "and then I will see the porter about the ventilators."

He omitted the first part of this, but fulfilled the last. The porter came, opened ventilators and put out lamps. Bessie tore off her heavy coverlet, and in less time than she could have thought possible after the car grew quiet, she was sound asleep, and remained so till morning, without being able to report whether the man snored or not.

WATER-CARRIER.

CHAPTER XXXV.

MAXIMILIAN.

WHEN Bessie awoke in the morning, it was with a strange, puzzled feeling about the way she had passed the night. The train was still rumbling along, and when she peeped out of the window, by lifting a corner of the thick shade over it, she saw that they were rushing along through a dreary country in the dim dawn. The car was perfectly silent; not even the gnome-like porter had begun his stealthy morning tour through the sleeping palace. She went to sleep again, and was roused a good deal later by the bustle of people sitting about her. The gnome came and said that breakfast would be at Silao, in half an hour. While she was dressing, as best she could, in a doubled-up position behind her curtains, she heard Mr. Pastor calling Tom, who was in the compartment opposite her, — "Hurry up! here is Irapuato in a moment!"

Bessie did not know what this meant, but she was ready, when the train stopped, to join Mr. Pastor on the platform, and Tom followed. A crowd of dark men in white garments beset the train, with their hands full of little baskets of delicious strawberries, — large, long, pointed, pale-tinted strawberries, heaped on each other, fresh from their beds, with the hulls on.

"Buy all you want," said their wise companion, "for this is the only place for them."

Bessie and Tom bought wildly of several delighted merchants, and carried their fragrant spoil into the car. The strawberries lasted through that day, and the next; they were so ripe and fresh that no sugar was needed, and they could be eaten like the plums of Jack Horner, with finger and thumb.

At Irapuato, these delicious strawberries are sold every day in the year to passengers on the trains.

When the party met at Silao, round the breakfast-table, the ladies found they had missed, during the night, several interesting things. In the first place, the Tajo de Nochistongo, the great cut through the hills, made to drain the city of Mexico in the seventeenth century. Tom and Mr. Pastor had seen it from the end of the last car, in dim moonlight, as they smoked their cigars before going to bed. The ladies reproached them for not calling them.

"You were just settled into quiet after putting Helena to bed, and I thought you would not care to be stirred up again," said Tom ; "but the cut was weird and strange in the dim light as we crept slowly along the edge of it."

The city suffered so much from inundations, that as early as 1607, the Marquis of Salinas, Spanish viceroy, gave orders for the beginning of a colossal work, cutting a subterranean canal or tunnel to drain the lakes by directing the little river Cuautitlan, from its course. This cut was called the *desagué* de Huehuetoca, a little village near the hills of Nochistongo. Hundreds of Indians toiled upon the work for nearly a year, and as they worked, many are said to have died from fatigue and rough treatment.

Operations were begun with great pomp, mass was said, the viceroy gave the first stroke with his spade. The canal proved too small ; many schemes were tried, and vast sums expended to enlarge and strengthen it. Different counsels, in all the years since, have prevailed, and the great canal has never been entirely completed, though millions have been spent upon it. However, the limits of the surrounding lakes were reduced by it, and the lake of Tezcoco, no longer receiving their contributions, was greatly diminished ; so that with the danger of inundation, water and vegetation likewise disappeared, leaving marshy, or sterile lands where formerly was sparkling water dotted with the canoes of the Indians. The Central Railroad has availed itself of the old work for its track, which runs close by the side of the cutting.

In the night, they had passed Tula, the ancient Toltec capital, which that ancient people began to build in 648. The Toltecs abandoned their city in 1051; the Chichimecs possessed it until 1196, when the Mexicans entered, and retained it over a hundred years, before they founded Tenochtitlan.

Bessie was quite cast down to find she had missed a glimpse of the home of the mysterious shadowy Toltecs, whose history vaguely underlies that of later Mexican races. Mr. Pastor persuaded her that Tula would have looked from the train, much like all the other towns they were flitting through. The maidens of Tula are said to be remarkable for beauty and picturesque costume.

They had passed, at dawn, Celaya, famous for its many churches, and shining domes. This is also a station on the National railroad, whose line going north here crosses the track of the Central.

But above all they had passed through Querétaro, and missed buying a delicious kind of nougat for which that town is famous. Mr. Pastor, who knew all the little dodges of Mexican travel, had arranged the night before with the Gnome, to buy a quantity of this truly delicious *dulce*. It is in long bars, made of nuts set in a sweet paste. The porter reported in the morning unfavorably, and returned a handful of pesos to the gentleman. All Querétaro was sound asleep when the train shot through it at three or four o'clock, and all the dulce-sellers were sharing that sweet repose, dreaming of possible bargains on future day-trains without a thought of the one they were then losing.

Querétaro has a more serious interest, as the spot where the unfortunate Emperor Maximilian closed his career, and Bessie had a fine chance during the long hours of this first day, as they rode over miles and miles of level, arid country, to impress upon the

DISTANT TULA.

MAXIMILIAN.

children the historical importance of the place, and to bring up to date the recent history of the country they were leaving. They knew nothing about it after the war with the United States in 1847. In May, 1848, at Querétaro, the treaty was ratified between Mexico and the United States. After this time, one President followed another with the usual new *pronunciamientos* and constitutions.

In 1858, Benito Juarez became President; he was the eighteenth. He was a true patriot; for eight years he directed with a firm hand the liberal party of his country, bringing to it the chance for rest and peace, and a rule of order.

He was an Aztec Indian, without a drop of Spanish blood, who had risen by his own merits to be Chief Justice. He drew up a constitution for his country, modeled upon that of the United States, but his chief struggle was against the political power of the Roman church. It was under his rule that the church was disestablished, and its property secularized; that is, the nation took possession of the church wealth for the national good, to pay its armies

BENITO JUAREZ.

who were fighting for the liberty of the people, and to develop a system of popular education. Under the judicious government of Juarez and his liberal party, Mexico was in a fair way to govern itself after peaceful republican methods; but this was strangely interrupted by the interference of Roman Catholic influence.

Louis Napoleon had by this time made himself Emperor of France. He was a Roman Catholic, and so also was his wife, the beautiful Empress Eugénie. The Pope, Pius the Ninth, who naturally disliked to lose Mexico, always hitherto a Catholic country, and to see the vast wealth administered by its churches diverted to other purposes, persuaded the French emperor to do something about it. They looked about for a good Catholic prince who would go to Mexico and put down the people, and restore the power of the church.

Maximilian, Arch-duke of Austria, and brother of the reigning Emperor, Francis Joseph, allowed himself to be used as the instrument of the church. His wife, Carlotta, was the daughter of the King of the Belgians. Probably they both thought it was a fine thing to come out to a savage country in the West and play emperor and empress. They packed up all their silver and splendid furniture, took crowns and robes and state-coaches, all exactly like princes and princesses in a fairy-tale; went to Rome for the Pope's blessing, and set sail for Mexico.

MAXIMILIAN.

All went well for a time, just as if some good fairy had arranged it for them. Louis Napoleon sent an army to fight for them, with a powerful general, Maréchal Bazaine, who quelled the soldiers of Juarez; the devout Catholics living in Mexico received them with rejoicing. They landed at Vera Cruz in the end of May, 1864, and entered the city of Mexico soon after, never dreaming, apparently, that the people did not want them, — probably not thinking at all about the people, but of the fine time they were going to have playing at emperor. They established themselves in splendor, began to adorn Chapultepec, instituted the order of the Mexican Eagle, and drove about in their state-coach.

But Louis Napoleon was not a good fairy. He knew very well that the only reason his little game of emperors was allowed to go on in Mexico was because the United States were busy with their Civil War, and could not attend to the misfortunes of their neighbors. At that time, the Government at Washington was fully occupied with the war between North and South; and although, as Republicans, the United States sympathized with the Mexicans, and resented the invasion there of a French army, to install an Austrian Emperor, President Lincoln could give nothing but sympathy in response to the appeals of Juarez. This state of things had to last until the Civil War was over. Soon after the fall of Richmond, and the end of the Southern Confederacy, a few plain words from Washington to the French Emperor informed him that he must withdraw his troops from Mexico, or all friendly relations would cease between the United States and France.

Louis Napoleon obeyed. He did not want a war with the United States, then full of valor and provided with a strong army, victorious after a long struggle. The French general, Bazaine, went away from Mexico with his troops, and left poor Maximilian to fight it out alone. He was persuaded to stay, flattered into the belief that he could hold his own with a volunteer force till help came from Austria. But no such help was forthcoming. The United States had no need to interfere, for the people of Mexico decided their own destiny. The emperor left the capital, and President Juarez returned to it, after an absence of about three years.

CARLOTTA.

The decisive blow was struck at Querétaro, where the emperor had taken up his headquarters in a convent. He surrendered, was tried by court-martial, found guilty, and condemned to die. He was executed on the nineteenth of June, 1867.

Carlotta, the unfortunate empress, returned home to her people. She went mad under the strain of such terrible experiences. She is still living, and, it is said, is now in better health, though not sound in mind.

It is impossible not to feel profound sympathy for the fate of these two people, lured into a trap from which they could not escape, by the treachery of others, and by their own infatuation. Maximilian was born too late. He dreamed of an old-fashioned empire, where pomp and splendor should prevail. He found a modern republic. His sceptre was struck down by a bayonet; his glass coach was no better than a pumpkin.

"I have heard it said," said Miss Lejeune, "that Juarez was a direct descendant of Montezuma."

"Yes," replied Bessie, "so have I. I wonder if it is so," she added dreamily, "and if Maximilian were a direct descendant of the Emperor Charles the Fifth,— it might be said that,—" She paused, and did not finish the sentence.

"Wonderful!" exclaimed Miss Lejeune.

THE EXECUTION OF MAXIMILIAN.

CHAPTER XXXVI.

OVER THE BORDER.

PRESIDENT JUAREZ was again elected President, having entered the capital among enthusiastic acclamations. He governed the country with firmness until his death, in 1872.

Mexico in these later years, in spite of revolutions and changes of popular feeling, is steadily advancing toward a settled prosperity. General Porfirio Diaz, who was in command of the Mexican army, before Querétaro, is now for the second time President of the Republic, since the expiration of the term December 1, 1884, of Manuel Gonzales, twenty-fifth President. The railroad lines spreading over the country, bringing it nearer to the United States, and promoting traffic, intercourse, and intelligent travelling, are helping the energetic efforts of wise and liberal statesmen of Mexico to put their country on a level with the most prosperous and civilized nations in the world.

Meanwhile it has not lost the flavor of romance and picturesque charm requisite to make it interesting.

As the party sat day after day trundling over the rails of the Mexican Central, there was plenty of time to talk of these things, and Bessie had ample chance to fill up the gaps, as well as she could, in the disjointed narrative she had been giving the children about Mexico, new and old.

It was strange how soon they fell into the routine of railway life, and how pleasant they found it,— how short the days were, flitting along as the train was flitting by large, modern towns with every indication of prosperity, or long tracts of arid land, where there was no sign of any town. Sometimes for hours the only landmarks, so to speak, were the stations, solidly built little structures, with a platform, the land around marked and crossed by tracks of wheels, and indented with hoof-marks. Generally a group of people were collected to meet the train. One or two men on horseback, and a rude diligence wagon waiting to carry its unfrequent passengers over the sandy track to some distant town, for which was the nearest station. But this was as they went farther and farther from the capital and civilized centres. They passed through many stirring towns, some of them celebrated for their mines, since the time of the conquest and before. Of course Bessie wanted to stop at all of them. Zacatecas looked especially interesting, as they wound about it upon the sides of steep hills, and Mr. Pastor tantalized her by accounts of Guanajuato, built all up and down stairs, which is reached by a branch from Silao.

GENERAL MANUEL GONZALES.

There was always something to see from the windows; they read but little, although little piles of books came out each day from the portmanteaus, and returned there at night.

One occupation never failed this healthy group of travellers;

this was discussing their meals. As soon as breakfast was over, Jack, who kept tight hold of the time-table, searched in the list for the place for the next repast. Breakfast was marked with *A*, close to the number indicating the time of arrival at the station where it would be served. *B* signified dinner, and *C* stood for supper. As the train approached one of these favored stations where food was to be had, every one was ready for a start; it seldom happened that any member of the party was missing, although Miss Lejeune generally thought beforehand she should omit the third meal of the day.

It was not the pangs of starvation which thus drove them forth, but a desire to see the kind of meal which would be prepared, for each time it was different,—de-

GENERAL PORFIRIO DIAZ.

lightful for some occult excellence or amusing for absolute dreadfulness.

At first there was a table-d'hôte at every station, where dishes were served by waiters, with a change of plate at every course,— with a good deal of confusion, but some attempt at system. Later on the restaurants were nothing but box-cars prematurely shunted off on a siding. The party climbed up wooden steps to enter, and were fed by a perfectly incompetent woman, who had herself probably cooked an immense quantity of things, and piled them pell-mell on top of one another on the table, for every one to pounce on what he liked. Many of the things were good, — early peas, string-beans, lettuce, chicken, beef,—the meats pretty tough, however. Sometimes a Chinaman hovered about the table; it would be a wrong use of words to say he waited upon it.

This first period lasted from Wednesday night till Saturday morning, when the Horners crossed the Rio Grande, entered their native land, and left the Mexican Central Railway, with regret at parting with their friendly Gnome, and all the pleasant officials of the train, and a strong feeling of sadness at going away from the picturesque country they had but gained a glimpse of.

At El Paso del Norte, on the Mexican side of the Rio Grande, they had their last Mexican meal, and paid away their last small pieces of Mexican money for bunches of sweet pink roses sold by ragged brown *muchachos*.

On the other side of the river, all was changed. The Aztec disappeared, and the Yankee reigned in his stead. Small darkskinned, black-haired, barefooted boys with gleaming teeth, clothed in rags, were no more to be seen, while prim little citizens of the United States walked the platform in jacket and trousers, boots and straw hats.

Domes and towers of pretty churches surrounded by adobe huts suddenly vanished, and clapboard houses, painfully new, painted glaring white or red, with green bindings, stood in their place.

But on they went, only exchanging one palace for another, after a rest of two or more hours in the waiting-room of the Atchison, Topeka and Santa Fé Railroad, which joins the Mexican Central at that point. They passed through the smallest possible piece of Texas, and then went through New Mexico, near Santa Fé, the southeastern corner of Colorado, and across the whole of Kansas to Kansas City.

They were full of mourning for the loss of the picturesque, which they had indeed utterly left behind them on the border, but they were fain to console themselves with the manifold signs of thrift and prosperity on every side; and they were genuinely amazed at the immense extent of their own country, and the swift march of civilization upon its ever extended border. They wauld have liked to stop at many places on the route, but their inexorable telegram, "Come home directly," ever sounded in their ears, and made them deaf to the call of Manitou and the South Park.

"It seems a pity, now we are here," said Miss Lejeune, "that we should not see a little more of the West, and be done with it. I feel as if I never should be here again, but really, rushing through the country in this way we gain no idea of the peaks and cañons and wonders we are always reading about."

"I know it," replied Bessie, "but do you know, I have been feeling rather glad we were obliged not to stop anywhere. My thoughts are so full of Mexican things, I do not feel equal to a new set of sensations."

"But, aunt Dut," said Tom, "you will come here with me sometime. I have a great mind to have a ranch and raise cattle here somewhere, and you might keep house for me; see, in just such a house as that!"

He pointed out a peculiarly forlorn and new-looking house in the outskirts of a very small new town.

"My dear!" was Miss Lejeune's only reply; but it was accompanied by an expressive glance of denial.

After a day, however, their pining for Mexico wore off, and they were ready to admire and approve all the triumphs of energy and industry of the great West. They passed through the lands inhabited by the little prairie-dogs, and saw several of them sitting on their holes, more like squirrels than dogs. The story is that each of these little animals shares his underground houses, each with an owl and a serpent. The children looked in vain for these boarders; they saw none of them, only the pleasant little proprietors sitting outside; perhaps the others were within.

This was the first week in May, and the country was lovely with early spring tints so delicate and delicious wherever they are.

A TRANSIENT PASSENGER.

The light greens and yellows of the tender trees were enhanced by a rosy flush from the "red-bud" which our New Englanders had never seen before.

It was strange to come upon these beginnings of verdure only three days after leaving the peaks and hillsides of Mexico nestling into mature dark-green foliage. The weather too was colder than their equable Mexican climate; the cars were heated by pipes without which they would have been too cold, but with which they were uncomfortably hot.

Still they went along very well. The ins and outs of different fellow passengers occupied them much. Bessie quoted,

> For men may come and men may go
> But I go on for ever.

They were the only through-passengers, and those who abode with them for a night and day only, seemed absurdly transient. They felt as if these must regard them as a part of the train perhaps, just as the Gnome was, so permanent were their habits, and so much were they at home in their compartments. For although they changed cars four times during the journey, each new one seemed soon exactly like the last, the differences were so slight. Even the Gnome seemed always the same friendly, amiable being; by the end of the journey they regarded him as an old, long-tried friend, and, in his latest form, ascribed to him all the attributes of each successive shape into which his essence had been cast.

CHAPTER XXXVII.

COLONEL INGHAM.

IT was on their second day in Kansas that, as they came into the palace from the elaborate breakfast to which they had given the better part of twenty minutes, a gentleman who had sat at the table behind them joined them most cordially and introduced himself.

"I felt sure it was you," said he, "all through breakfast, and yet I was afraid to speak. Not that I have seen most of you, since you rode upon my knee, or since, Miss Bessie, I gave you your first lesson in horseback riding on my foot."

Miss Lejeune turned to him with surprise, and said, "Is it possible?"

It was possible, and this gentleman who then and there joined their party for the day, proved to be Colonel Ingham.

He sent the porter into the parlor car in which he had just established himself, and bade him bring back the larger of his two portmanteaus. So soon as this arrived, he opened it, and interested Jack and Helena for a long time in showing them specimens of various ores which he had collected in Arizona and which he was carrying home. Indeed he gave them some choice pieces for the museum which it was understood they were one day to form.

"Indeed," said he, "Bessie, your father is a good deal changed, if this carbonate does not interest him. He will tell you a story which will take your hair off your head about a specimen of which this will remind him."

When he found they had all been travelling in Mexico, Colonel Ingham was very much interested. "The next time," he said, "you must let me know. Let us have six weeks if we cannot get two months, and we will go to New Mexico together, and you shall have time to see what there is to see.

"First of all, I will telegraph to our good friend Cushing that we are coming, and Mrs. Cushing shall have a lodging swept out for us in one of the actual four-story buildings which Coronado saw three centuries ago. The Zuni gentlemen dined at my house three or four years ago; very agreeable gentlemen they are, and I have been longing for a time when I might accept their invitations and test their hospitality.

"Then we will go out with our knapsacks and hammocks, and we will see how we should like to live as the cave-dwellers lived. Bessie, you shall make such a collection of pottery as shall shame your Mexican specimens, and the best you did in Spain."

The children were quite at ease with him now, and somebody asked who Coronado was.

Coronado was a Spanish gentleman who was put in command of the party which made the first exploration from the city of Mexico in these regions. News had come in from the most northern provinces then settled that a certain priest named Nizza, or Nica, had discovered a civilized community in the North, and that this nation had no end of turquoises, silver and gold. They lived in Seven Cities, he said.

Now all through the explorations of Columbus and the others, there had been a tradition of the Land of Seven Cities. When Cabot came back to Bristol before Columbus ever touched the mainland, it was said that Cabot had found the Land of the Seven Cities.

"Perhaps it was Aztlan," said Helena in her squeaky voice.

Colonol Ingham looked amazed to hear words of wisdom from so small a mouthpiece.

"Why, yes!" he replied. "It was always understood that the Land of the Seven Cities when found, was to be a very rich land. Nearly a generation had passed since Cortés took possession of Mexico. The first plunderings were well over, but with a very distinct memory remaining, and all the Spaniards in Mexico went wild to go to the Seven Cities. Coronado was fitted out with an expedition admirably equipped to go by land on the route indicated by this dying friar. An expedition was sent by sea to coöperate, up the Gulf of California which Cortés had discovered not long before. Coronado had to cross the whole open State of Arizona, and he did not find it any less desert than he would have found it to-day. When he came to the Seven Cities, he found houses or palaces three stories high, as the friar had said, but he found of turquoises very few, and he found very little gold and silver. He had some fighting with the Indians, or Aztecs, if Aztecs they were; and powder and ball did what they always do. But as for courage, they had quite as much as he had, and one might say the same of their discipline, perhaps. They fought for their homes, and they fought very well. However, Coronado wintered there, and he sent out an expedition the next spring to the eastward to see if he could not strike the Gulf of Mexico, or the ocean. This expedition crossed the prairies as far as the Missouri River.

"It was not," said Colonel Ingham, "very far from this very line on which we are riding, that they rode East and West that summer. They met very few people; they saw the enormous herds of buffaloes which for centuries were the monarchs of these regions; day after day they rode, and they rode over countries without a tree, and at last, having found no ocean, they turned and they rode back again. If you would get out, Jack, and dig where we crossed that little creek just now, I am not sure but you might find a Spanish helmet, or the hilt of a Spanish sword. Such things have been found there, and the Kansas Historical Society will show them to us in its museum, if Miss Lejeune likes to stop over a day and rest, and buy herself a new ribbon in Topeka."

There was a chance here for some little talk about their haste in returning, and Colonel Ingham for the first time had Jack and Helena explained to him.

"I took it for granted," said he, "that they were young Horners. There generally are some cropping up."

"I am the last," said Tom, with a smile.

Colonel Ingham was too full of his subject to dwell long on such trifles.

"It is sufficiently curious," he said, turning to Miss Lejeune, "that these very States which are the last added to the republic, and for that matter the last settled by our great and glorious Anglo-American family, should run back into written history quite as far as the farthest, and have indeed annals more picturesque and romantic than the wisest of us old stagers can digest out of the records of town meetings in Dudley's day and Winthrop's. You have to turn an old windmill at Newport into a Norseman's watch-tower, if you want to have anything legendary at hand, while you had all the time waiting for you here an architecture and a civilization primeval as far as you know, and certainly individual and national.

"I rather think, that if you were to look through Humboldt's account of Mexico, you would find him sniffing at Coronado's exaggerations. And now that we are on the spot, it proves that Coronado was as accurate a historian as we have in the whole series from dear Columbus down.

"I dare say Mr. Horner has told you how I showed him,— by the way, were you not all in Spain at the same time?"

"Yes," said Bessie, "but don't you remember, we all missed you except papa, because we were at Aranjuez?"

"Ah? It was in the Academy of History,— a pen-and-ink drawing of a buffalo which one of Coronado's sergeant-majors made, which was really, Miss Lejeune, quite as good as I should make to-day."

Miss Lejeune said, what was the exact truth, that she had forgotten Colonel Ingham had anything to do with the buffalo, but that Mr. Horner had shown her the picture, and she had made a tracing of it which she had somewhere in her scrap-book.

"I had these Zuni gentlemen at my house, as I told the children," said he. "Their business in Boston, if you remember, was to renew their supply of salt water. They had kept what they had for religious purposes for two or three hundred years, and their stock was running short. My good friend Cushing had brought them to the East to renew their supply. The Mayor took them down the bay to Deer Island, and they filled some demijohns from the rising sea, then and there shipped by Adams's Express for them towards their home. Such are the conveniences of modern civilization. They bade me good-by, and I bade them good-by. I went across to Paris, and that was the year I ran across you in Madrid. Of course I was interested in all this, and the first day I was there, I went into the Academy of History, and by good luck ran against Horner, consoling himself for your absence. Those people are very civil, and they produced the manuscripts of the collections which dear old Munoz made for his book which he never wrote. I looked at the index, and I told them that they might give me the eightieth volume, which was the volume for 1542. I opened the book, Miss Lejeune, and almost the first thing I lighted on was this, — I have it copied in this pocketbook, because I showed it to Captain Rourke yesterday." And Colonel Ingham eagerly translated from the Spanish:

"'They offer rites and sacrifices to certain idols; but that which they worship most of all is Water, to which they offer little painted straws, and feathers, and bunches of yellow flowers.'

"Now there is the report of a man whom it was convenient to

sniff at for two or three hundred years because nobody had been after him to verify his observation!

"Acoma; we must go to Acoma together. Tom and Bessie, you will make a better business going to Acoma than I shall. When you come to Acoma it is on the top of a cliff, some six hundred feet, I think, above you. I forgot how many ladders there are, Bessie, but I think seventeen; and each ladder takes you up thirty or forty feet. When you wake up in the morning, after you have had your breakfast, you go down the ladders and you hoe your corn, see to your squashes, or attend to any other duty that comes next your hand. If you find you have forgotten a rake or a trowel, you go back for it over the ladders, and come down again. When you feel as if you had worked enough you go back over the ladders and have your supper and go to bed. As for dinner, I am not certain whether you go back for that or whether you eat it on the plain below. All the houses are up there, all the fields are down below.

"Now, my dear Miss Lejeune," said the Colonel eagerly, "all this was described better than I describe it to you more than two hundred years ago, by some Spanish gentlemen who were sent up there or went as volunteers. But if you will reflect, apartment houses had not then been invented; the best you could do in Edinburgh in the way of high houses were only seven stories high, and all this story of Acoma was turned over as a lie, just as Mandeville's and Marco Polo's were. But one fine day, some of our people happened along there, and lo! the Acoma people were going up and down their ladders just as they had been for two centuries, and just as if nobody had scratched them out of the book; and they are going up and down their ladders to-day. They are all citizens of the United States now, and I hope they all voted for Mr. Blaine last November. I believe they call the place Acuco now, and I will not swear that the ladders have not been removed, but it is the same place which the Spanish gentlemen saw."

Colonel Ingham's advent and his Spanish stories quite waked up Jack and Helena, who had often heard of him, and who were always a little confused as to what age of the world he belonged to. His eagerness now seemed to bring the Spanish adventurers close to them.

CHAPTER XXXVIII.

KANSAS.

KANSAS is so large a State that one of their Governors boasted, a few years ago, that every man, woman and child in the United States could have a separate standing-place given him in Kansas, and they should all be so far from each other that they could not talk to each other.

This is literally true, unless you call it talking when a person is shouting loud enough to hail the main-top. For if you will make the calculation Kansas could give an acre of land to every person in the United States, and would still have a good many acres to spare. Now you may put Strephon in the middle of a square-acre lot, and Chloe in the middle of the next, and Chloe will not hear much of what Strephon says to her, particularly if a northwest wind is blowing against his voice. And Strephon with the advantage of the wind will not hear much of what Chloe says in reply.

From the western end of this Kansas to the eastern end, the Horners rode. They rode and they rode as Coronado's men did three hundred and fifty years before, on their Spanish horses. People say that some of those gallant steeds then and there ran away, and that that is the reason why, eighty years ago, Philip Nolan and his friends found so many wild horses in Texas, and why there were so many on these very prairies. This is probably so, for strange to say, the fossil horses which Professor Marsh and others find a little to the north of here were not bigger than dogs, and they had three toes, almost as if they were birds. Now Philip Nolan's horses and the famous horse smuggler, who is one of these Kansas horses, or has their blood in him, have very good hoofs, and are not like dogs at all.

They rode and they rode all one night and all one day, and in the afternoon they were done with Kansas, and swept into the State of Missouri. But the name held to them still, for they found that though they were in Missouri, they were still in Kansas City.

It is one of the largest and most prosperous cities of the West. There is an immense business in cattle carried on there, and several of the great lines of travel and of freight meet here. But thirty years ago, as Mr. Pastor and Colonel Ingham told them, it was an insignificant frontier town.

When they arrived in the station, they were to leave their well-beloved Atchison and Topeka Railroad, which had brought them so happily and well all the way from El Paso. It proved that they had two or three hours before the Eastern train started, and all parties gladly consented to a walk under the pilotage of Colonel Ingham and Mr. Pastor.

As they left the station, the runners from the different hotels solicited them, but Colonel Ingham shook his head good-naturedly, and as they passed one and another of the fine buildings, he said laughingly to Miss Lejeune, " I wish I knew which of these hotels I owned once!"

"How did you own it?" she asked, surprised.

"Well, in truth," said he, " I only owned, I suppose, one undivided thousandth part of it. But the first time I ever heard of Kansas City, was when I and mine bought a hotel here, acting under the advice of this same Governor Robinson whom we could not see this afternoon because we did not stop at Lawrence.

"There is romance for the children, and adventure which will quite compare with Castaneda or Coronado." For Tom had been complaining that in our times there is no chance for such chivalry as theirs. "I will tell the children about it as we ride through Missouri," he said, "and before we come out on the Mississippi, I shall have a chance to tell it long."

Bessie said that she remembered as a child hearing of "bleeding Kansas," "starving Kansas," and "fighting Kansas," but that it seemed peaceful enough now."

"Yes," said Ingham, rather pensively, "but that is because of these brave men and brave women who came here summoned by an idea. There has never been, dear Miss Lejeune, a more spirited emigration since time began, if by spirited you imply the inspiration of brave men and women."

Miss Lejeune said that the first public meeting she remembered was a meeting she went to about the Nebraska bill. She remembered that Henry Wilson spoke, and Charles Francis Adams.

This little talk of theirs led up to their telling the story to the children after dinner that evening, as they shot through the valley of the Missouri up toward Iowa in the palace of the C. B. and Q. C. B. and Q. being interpreted, means Chicago, Burlington and Quincy.

Sometimes Colonel Ingham talked, sometimes Miss Lejeune, and so the children had the history from the lips of those who had seen, or who remembered.

As long ago as 1820, before any of them were born, there was a long and fierce struggle in Congress about the admission of the State of Missouri into the Union,—whether the people of that State might hold slaves or no. In the Northern and Middle States, slavery had been abolished; in the States north of the Ohio and east of the Mississippi, it had never existed. The Northern people led, and were led, by Rufus King, Daniel Webster and other natural leaders, who determined that the new State should not be permitted to maintain slavery. But the settlers already there had negro slaves, and all the Southern States of the Union declared that their people could not emigrate into Missouri, if they were not permitted to carry their slaves with them. They said it would be unjust to them to keep them out of the new State.

The reason why this had not been settled before, was that the United States did not own any territory west of the Mississippi, until the purchase of all that region from Napoleon, in 1803.

The Missouri controversy raged through 1819 and the beginning of 1820. The Southern people even declared that they would divide the Union if they were not permitted to take their slaves into the new State. At last the thing was settled by what was called the Missouri Compromise. This was the first of a series of "Compromises," devised by Henry Clay. It provided that Missouri might be a slave State. But it also provided that this was on condition that all lands north of the parallel which made the southern line of Missouri should, when the time came, be made free States; all lands south of that line were to have slaves if the people wished.

Under this compromise things went on for a generation. Iowa and Wisconsin on the North, were admitted as free States, Arkansas and Florida were admitted as slave States. With the annexation of Texas, in 1845, the contest had been renewed; but Congress and President Tyler had then determined that slavery should be permitted there.

Under this compromise, things worked along until 1854. Some of the people in Western Missouri then began to wish to go over into the region west of that State. They had already persuaded Congress to add to Missouri the large fertile triangle east of the Missouri River through which the Horners were riding for a little while after they left Kansas City. This annexation had been in violation of the Missouri Compromise, and perhaps it gave some confidence to the settlers in Missouri who wanted more. Somehow or other, they determined to have a territory made west of Missouri, which they proposed at first to call the Nebraska Territory, from the name of the great Nebraska or Platte River, which runs from the Rocky Mountains eastward to the Missouri.

Just as if there had been no Missouri Compromise, they proposed that all this territory should be open to the institution of slavery.

Observe, the precise condition on which the Northern States had assented to the existence of slavery in Missouri, Arkansas and Florida, was that it should not be permitted in this very region north of the parallel of thirty-six degrees, thirty minutes.

It was a time when the Southern statesmen had everything very much their own way. Perhaps some of them thought this plan would slip through without opposition. But, in fact, it proposed the distinct violation of public faith. And it struck the first blow for the movement which ended in the Civil War, in the emancipation of the slaves, and in the reconstruction of the Union.

By another attempt at a sort of compromise, the "Nebraska Bill," so called, was amended in Congress, so as to provide that the first settlers on the ground should determine whether they would have slaves or no. This was called "squatter sovereignty," in the language of those times.

"'And it was then and there," said Colonel Ingham, when they came to this part of the story, "that I came to own an undivided thousandth part of a hotel in Kansas City. For we formed at once in New England, under the leadership of Eli Thayer, an 'Emigrant Aid Company.' That company sent the first organized body of emigrants into Kansas, — a plucky set, who had fighting enough to do before all was over. I was a director in that company. When we had only thirty thousand dollars to spend, all the newspapers here in Missouri, which were all given to lying, said we had five million. This was a good thing for us, for next to being rich it is well to be thought so. We sent this Charles Robinson I tell you of, a wise, brave, prudent, shrewd man, to say where this first colony should go. He came out here and selected the site of Lawrence, which was named after Mr. Amos Lawrence, who was active in the enterprise. Then and there was it that this Doctor Robinson, as we called him then, selected a tavern in Kansas City and bought it for our company, so that we might have a place in Missouri, where our people could rendezvous before they made the adventure of the new territory. There were certain Indian claims upon that pleasant valley land between Lawrence and Kansas City, and the site of Lawrence was the first site open to settlement. To that spot, Charles Robinson took the first colony in the next spring. There they lived, there they fought, there, before the Civil War was over, many of them were killed. There is no more horrible story than that of the massacre of Lawrence, when, in cold blood at daylight, one morning, every man left in the town was killed at his own door or in his own bed by an invasion of border ruffians.

"On the other hand, in face of every form of lying and treachery on the part of the general government, and of every persecution on the part of a few of the fire-eaters here, those settlers fought their way through. By the time the Civil War came, they were ready to be admitted into the Union as a free State. They were all used to fighting, and they furnished more men for the army in proportion to their number than any other State, old or new, North or South. They went through horrible sufferings from droughts, from famines and locusts, and I know not what, but they had the root of the matter in them. By and by it proved that the American Desert of the old maps was not to be a desert, after all. In fullness of time, came along the Atchinson and Topeka Railroad, beneficently carrying the emigrants out and sending their corn and wheat, and barley and oats, and silk and peaches, and everything else that the heart of man can desire, to those parts of the world that want them.

"Any man you met yesterday would tell you that there is no

State in America which does so much every day to serve the good God in answering that little daily prayer of his children, 'Give us this day our daily bread,' as does this same State of Kansas which was 'starving Kansas,' only twenty five years ago.

"I do not know what these Illinois people would say to that, or what the Iowa people would say, but I think the Kansas people are probably right.

"But for my part, I do not love them so much for the silk or the honey, or the corn, or the oats, but because their fathers and mothers, these people who are as old as you and I, Miss Lejeune, had the courage of their convictions and were true to an idea."

CHAPTER XXXIX.

STILL MOVING.

AT Chicago, Colonel Ingham left them, as suddenly as he had appeared, with a cordial shake of the hand all round, but no sort of account of where he had been or where he was going next. Jack was beginning to put a whole catechism of questions about him, when the appearance of Tom, with a bright smile on his face, and a yellow telegram in his hand, silenced the boy.

They had, by this time, changed cars once more, and were passing the south shore of Lake Michigan, on the "Lake Shore and Michigan Southern." Tom had gone off with Colonel Ingham, and now returned alone in ample time before the start.

He handed the telegram to Miss Lejeune, and Bessie looked over her shoulder, while the children watched and wondered.

"Oh! I am so thankful," murmured Miss Lejeune.

"I have been hoping so, all along," said Bessie.

"What is it?" cried Jack. "Is mamma coming to meet us?" His face was lighted up by his guess.

"My dear boy," said Miss Lejeune, "we did not want to tell you that your mamma has been very ill. That was why we were hurrying so. But this telegram says she is out of danger, and so we need not be alarmed about her."

Jack wanted now to know all about it. There was but little to tell. While Miss Augusta explained to him the news they had received in Mexico just before starting, Bessie asked her brother how he came to have the telegram.

"As soon as were sure of the time we should arrive here, I

telegraphed to Clarence, and he sent his answer to the care of the ticket-master here. See, it is dated this morning!"

"Oh! how quick it seems," cried Bessie, "and just like Clarence's own voice! I could eat that telegram!"

"I thought," said Tom, "you would still prefer to keep on, instead of stopping for Niagara Falls."

"Oh dear me, yes!" cried Miss Lejeune. "I am so in this way of life, I could go on forever."

"So I telegraphed back that we should arrive to-morrow evening," continued Tom.

"To-morrow evening! does it seem possible!"

Colonel Ingham's talk had made the day before go like lightning. They missed him now, and their dear Mr. Pastor, who also left them at Chicago. His constant attention to the ladies, and his pleasant ways with the children, had made him a great favorite. Everybody lamented his absence.

But their lives were taking on a gray, monotonous tone, which small events could brighten or dull but little. The hours rolled out behind them, like the straight lines of the track behind the car, losing their individuality in a long ribbon sliding off into the distance.

The ladies bore it very well. The worst thing was dressing in the morning, and waiting their turn for the use of the one small dressing-room, which is used by all the ladies of the car. Bessie's plan was to leave her sleeper preternaturally early while every one else was sound asleep, so as to manage a difficult and perilous bath in the set basin before any one else wanted it.

Once, by good luck, there were water faucets in the stateroom occupied by Miss Lejeune and Helena, but only once. Then it was tiresome, after rising so early, to wait an hour or more for breakfast; it was inconvenient to have to keep all one's things locked up in a portmanteau under the seat, or scattered about upon it, to be packed every night when the seat was turned into a bed.

But they bore it very well, and sought what variety they might find in popping out at the stations for a hasty walk on the platform, or hanging over the rear end of the car to catch a glimpse of the towns they passed through. Occasionally they changed their positions by going to sit in another car, where the air was somewhat fresher, and the arm-chairs at least different, if not more comfortable than their own seats.

They were at Buffalo for breakfast on Wednesday morning, and had it in the restaurant attached to the station. All the time between Kansas City and Chicago, meals had been served in a dining-room car on the train, at little tables by large windows, where they could enjoy the flying scenery while they did justice to the excellent fare provided.

"On the whole," said Miss Lejeune, "I prefer to be sitting still while I am dining. It is too distracting to eat at the rate of thirty miles an hour."

When they were fixed for the morning in their seats, the ladies both knitting, the children at the windows, and Tom walking up and down the car with his hands in his pockets, he stopped before his sister and said.

"Bessie, do you think you have done you duty by Montezuma and Cortés and their relations towards Jack and Helena?"

"I do not know that I could have bored them any more about the Conquest," said Bessie, laughing good-naturedly.

"You have not bored us at all," said Jack, with his eyes bright, "and I know all about them now, although I was rather mixed up part of the time."

"Let us hear," said Tom; "Bessie, this boy reminds me more and more of Hubert."

"The Aztecs," said Jack, "were a very good sort of people that made their city on a rock, where there was a nopal and an eagle and a serpent. They came from a place away off called Aztlan, and perhaps Colonel Ingham has been there.

PACHUCA, ON THE ROUTE TO TAMPICO.

"They had a bloody, cruel religion, but they had beautiful feather clothes and a great many nice customs. Then Cortés came up there with his horses and cannons, and drove them all away, though at first they were more mighty than he was. But he tumbled down their ugly gods, and burnt up their pictures, and built a new city, and the land came to be full of Spaniards. And he died."

"And was buried a great many times," remarked Helena.

"Yes; and so the country was Spanish for a great while, until the people got tired of being Roman Catholics, and besides, of being governed by viceroys; and so they kept having revolutions and revolutions, until now they are just like the United States."

"But once Maximilian came in a glass coach to be Emperor," said Helena, "and they cut his head off."

"You cannot understand all about it," said Jack, with a superior air, "because you are a little girl."

As Helena's face clouded at this patronizing remark, Tom took Jack off with him to see some snow on the hillsides they were passing.

Bessie sighed. "I sometimes think," she said, "that it only makes prigs of children to talk to them of history and the things I am interested in, connected with travel. Perhaps they would enjoy themselves more, just simply observing naturally the places and people that come before them. I think I prefer Helena's notion of the glass coach, to Jack's superficial knowledge which makes him feel so superior to her."

"You are tired," replied Miss Lejeune, "or you would not talk in that fashion. Jack is not a prig, but a remarkably nice boy, and much nicer since you and Tom have had him in hand. When I first saw him last fall, with Marianne, he was all the time asking the most intolerable questions about what this was for, and why that was so. You have turned his inquiring mind into better channels. Of course his knowledge is superficial, but there is no harm in it, and if he follows his father's archæological turn, as I dare say he may, this foundation will be of service to him."

"Well, let us hope so," said Bessie. "As for Helena, I fear her recollections of Mexico will be but confused in the future."

She said this with a smile, turning to the little girl as she spoke.

"Mamma will say you must have your hair cut," she went on, brushing Helena's loose bang out of her eyes. It had grown very long during their journey, for no one had thought of cutting it, or else the confidence in Mexican hairdressers had not been sufficient to trust.

"You look like a little Aztec!" said Bessie. "But you have had a pretty nice journey, Helena, have you not?"

"What do you like best in Mexico, Helena?" asked Miss Lejeune.

"Red plums, and dulces, and tortillas," replied the little girl promptly.

Tortillas are thin flat cakes of corn, which is ground by hand, in a primitive manner, by the Indian women. The travellers often saw them at work preparing it under a tree by the roadside, with a little open-air fire at hand to cook with.

GRINDING CORN FOR TORTILLAS.

"What! nothing but things to eat! In all Mexico!" she exclaimed reprovingly.

"Oh! I thought you meant things to eat," she replied, stretching herself out upon the seat, and nestling her head down in Bessie's lap. "Let me see, next best, I think I like Popocatepetl and Is-tac-ci-huatl."

She was asleep before the last long word had drawled itself from her lips. She had borne the journey remarkably well, thanks to a nap she managed every afternoon; but it was evident, on this last day, that she was feeling the effect of the unusual confinement.

"Poor little thing!" said Miss Lejeune. "I shall be relieved when we hand her over to her mother."

"To-night, only to-night!" exclaimed Bessie; "can it really be true that we shall have travelled four thousand miles in a week, and that we shall be at home to-night!"

"I wonder why we feel as if we had been gone so long, when, in fact, this trip is the shortest we have ever made together."

"Is it not strange? Perhaps because Mexico is so near that we could go home any minute, if we did not keep deciding to stay away. I am glad it is so near the States, for it is a lovely playground for tired Americans. How easy for business-men to slip off by this through train, and in one week to find themselves in scenes utterly, wholly different from the field of their cares and worries." It was Bessie who said this.

"And such a climate!" added Miss Lejeune. "Burr! we have felt nothing like this since we left!"

She drew her wrap closely round her with a shiver, as some one threw open the door, letting in a piercing blast.

"Look! I do believe it is snowing!"

A few scattered flakes were falling.

CHAPTER XL.

CONCLUSION.

THE Mexican travellers arrived safely, and were warmly welcomed to the small but comfortable home of Mary Hervey, — her that was a Horner.

Mr. and Mrs. Horner were there, and Philip, who had come from Cambridge on purpose to meet them, was there, and Mrs. Johnstone, rapidly recovering from an attack of feverish prostration which had seized her on the voyage, so that Clarence Hervey, when he was summoned to meet her on the arrival of the steamer at the docks, had felt her to be in a most alarming condition, and after consultation with his family, sent off the telegram which brought them home so promptly.

Repose, kind care, and the attentions of the wise old family physician had immediate effect upon the poor worried invalid; and when Miss Lejeune in her dressing gown came to her bedside early, the morning after her arrival from Mexico, she found her propped up with pillows, and looking brighter and better than when they parted.

"O my dear!" she said, "I was so thankful to get home!"

"You poor Marianne!" said her friend. "You are certainly not cut out for a traveller."

"No, indeed!" replied the invalid, closing her eyes, and turning her head upon the pillow with a shudder. "Certainly not, in those countries. You have no idea, Augusta, how terrible it was at Merida!"

"No doubt," soothingly assented Miss Lejeune, while she secretly

A LAKE CITY.

did doubt ; for from all they had heard of Merida, it was a city most interesting and quite sufficiently comfortable; but it was not worth while to discuss the matter.

"And where is Minton?" she asked, a little severely.

"Minton is here," said Mrs. Johnstone, then added as a sort of apology, "she behaved very badly, but I could not turn her off entirely, you know, because she understands Baby so well. So when I found she really was determined to come, the only thing seemed to be for me to come too."

She was feeling round in the bed for her handkerchief, and her lips began to quiver.

Miss Lejeune desired nothing less at the moment than to discuss the subject of Minton's defection, and Mrs. Johnstone's flight, for she herself was ready to drop, after a broken night which could scarcely be called one of rest.

"You did quite right, my dear," she hastened to say, having indeed previously persuaded herself that Mrs. Johnstone's return was the best thing for every one, all considered; "you did quite right not to stay there alone, and you must not fret yourself with thinking about it. The dear children are perfectly well, and so happy to see mamma again. And now I must leave you and lie down, for my head is still rocking with the motion of the train."

Her head indeed was still rocking, and so was Bessie's ; and they continued to rock for several days. Jack and Helena slept steadily all through that day, with scarcely intermission for food, but on the second day they were bright and lively as usual, and ready to write letters to dear papa, and tell him all about the houses with ladders which they had learned from Colonel Ingham.

As for Bessie's first morning at home, she breakfasted in bed, where she was visited in turns by Mary, with the wonderful Horner baby, by her father before he went out for the day, and finally by her mother, who brought her breakfast, and sat by her for a long good comfortable chat.

Mrs. Horner looked older than when we first saw her several years ago. Her hair was sparsely gray, and a small cap was always perched upon her head. These caps were a source of trial to her daughters, as they seldom came up to the mark set before them as the ultimatum in caps.

Mrs. Hervey was always sending home caps from Broadway shops of distinction, but somehow these stayed in their cartons, while self-made ones, so to speak, appeared upon the maternal head. Mrs. Horner was a little touchy about her caps, and even Miss Lejeune, who scorned to wear any, seldom ventured any criticism.

"Well, my dear," said Mrs. Horner, "I am thankful to have you at home at last, and I think, by your letters, you cannot be sorry yourself. This Johnstone dispensation has been such a trial!"

"O, mamma, we have had a perfectly lovely time, and you must not exaggerate the Johnstone business. We were delighted to have the children, and aunt Dut has behaved wonderfully well."

"However," said Mrs. Horner, threading her needle with some difficulty, "I think it is well that your father and I did not go. We neither of us care for those tropical countries, and then the people are so uncivilized."

"Now, mamma," exclaimed Bessie, sitting up in bed, while her long hair tumbled down about her shoulders, "did you, or did you not, read our letters?"

Her mother looked quite alarmed. She put down the stocking she was mending,— one of Clarence Hervey's socks,— and said:

"Why, certainly, my dear, and we all said you never were more amusing and descriptive; but why do you ask with such violence?"

"Because, mamma, you are just like everybody else we have met since we came into the States. People go on persisting that Mexico is a savage country with a tropical climate, while we keep saying it is entirely civilized and that the climate is perfect!"

CONCLUSION.

"But you wrote about bananas, and about that place where there is malaria, Quotta, I think."

"But we did not go there!" cried poor Bessie. "Cuautla; and it is a very lovely place in the right season. Of course, if you choose to go and sit in a swamp surrounded by tall tropical plants, hung with boa-constrictors, you can do so, that is, if you go exactly opposite to all the directions given for intelligent travel in Mexico. But if your taste is in favor of a perfect climate, and no wild beasts, you can find it, somewhere in Mexico, at any season of the year."

"Of course, certainly," said Mrs. Horner. "I do not doubt it, my dear child. Your father and I, however, have been very comfortable this winter; we have both come to the conclusion that the climate of New York is about as good as any we have seen."

Bessie fell back in bed, and laughed feebly and dejectedly; she was too tired to discuss the matter, and she let it go, but her head, in spite of the thumping and rumbling going on in it, went over the times, countless in number, she had heard her mother, sitting on sunny balconies in warm climates, describe that of New York as the one thing on earth most desirable to avoid.

She was silent for a while, and her attention wandered from her mother's discourse. When she came back to it, it was about the wonderful accomplishments of the Hervey baby.

For so it was. The wandering days of the Horners were over. The parents were growing old; of this there could be no concealment. Their children were now all men and women, fitted, by travel and careful education, to take their own places in life, and with a tolerable knowledge of other countries, capable of becoming good citizens of their own.

Clarence Hervey, who used to carry a ticket for an oceansteamer passage always in his pocket, was now the most settled-down of men. He hated the word "plan;" and he carefully suppressed all prospectuses of Raymond excursions and all railway tables, lest they should stir the ancient blood of the once roving family into which he had married.

His own wife he could trust, for she never stirred from the house if she could help it; she kept house by postal-cards, did her shopping by proxy, and although she still sent to Paris for her dresses, to a quiet little *modiste* they had set up there long ago, seemed to have forgotten otherwise that any other continent than her own existed.

Mary Hervey was much changed in appearance from the slight girl of sixteen whom Mr. Hervey met first on a steamer bound for Europe. She was blooming now and matronly, and bade fair to become as buxom as her mother; that is to say, not too stout, but just enough not to be wiry. She was an admirable house-keeper, and kept up her simple establishment with that appearance of making no effort, which is only brought about by a great deal of thought, and constant vigilance behind the scenes.

As for Miss Lejeune, she everywhere announced that her travelling days were over. Her wicker trunk had tumbled to pieces, and her favorite sea-portmanteau was irredeemably broken up. She declared that she never should renew them; and that she meant to spread herself out in her old apartment, and spend the rest of her life arranging the things she had bought on her travels, and had never yet found time to take out of their packing cases.

Tom and Bessie looked on and listened in silence. They shared, neither of them, this lotos-eating wish for repose. They saw no reason why the whole Horner colony should not spend that very summer in Ireland which they had never seen, then pass up to Iceland, and come home perhaps round by Japan, across Russia.

"Must we wait," they said, "till the baby is grown up?"

However that may be, Bessie has bought a Russian grammar written in German; but Tom goes down town with his father every day, and thus leaves that gentleman more leisure for the baby.

QUIEN SABE?

CONCLUSION.

Mr. Johnstone pursues his researches in Yucatan, and writes thence wonderful archæological letters. To tell the truth, he seems not to miss his family overmuch, though he speaks in every letter of having Jack with him when he is done with school. The rest of the Johnstones are boarding in New York, and Minton looks after the family.

When the Horners meet next Christmas day, as they surely will, to eat the Christmas turkey together, Miss Lejeune, of course, present, as one of the family rather than a guest, they will "fight their battles o'er again," and revive many scenes and incidents of their travels, laughing over the funny episodes, discussing the chance companions, weighing the advantage of the different journeys. Miss Lejeune may quote, perhaps, —

> Surely, surely, slumber is more sweet than toil, the shore
> Than labor in the deep mid-ocean, wind and wave and oar;
> O rest ye, brother mariners, we will not wander more.

Nevertheless, while any part of the globe remains unexplored, the old flame, the old longing for travel may burst forth again. Bessie for one, and Tom for another, hope so.

Quien Sabe!

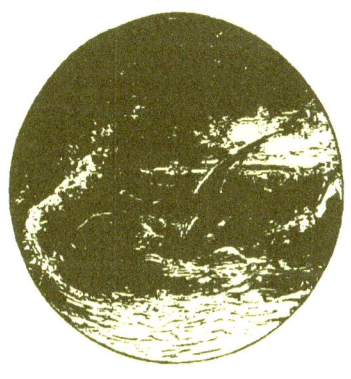

Books for Young Americans
By ELBRIDGE S. BROOKS
The Popular "True Story" Series

Seven 4to volumes of from 200 to 250 pages each, profusely illustrated and attractively bound in cloth, each $1.50.

"A series which contains the lives of Columbus, Washington, Lincoln, Grant, and Franklin, and worthy of hearty commendation. Every grown-up person who has read one of them will wish to buy the whole series for the young folks at home." — *The Christian Advocate.*

This series contains:

The True Story of Christopher Columbus, called the Admiral. Revised edition.

"With its thorough historical research and its novelty of treatment it is *the* Columbus book of its time." — *The Interior*, Chicago.

The True Story of George Washington, called the Father of His Country.

"Although many excellent biographies of our first President have been prepared for the young, we think that Mr. Brooks has presented the best, and has sustained well if not added to his reputation gained by his previous efforts in historical fields for young readers." — *S. S. Library Bulletin.*

The True Story of Abraham Lincoln, the American.

"His life reads like a romance, the best romance that ever was printed, and Mr. Brooks has done an admirable work. . . . The story of Lincoln was never more ably told." — *Evening Post*, Chicago.

The True Story of U. S. Grant, the American soldier.

"Carefully written in that style which makes Mr. Brooks so popular a writer with his young readers." — *The Pilgrim Teacher.*

The True Story of Benjamin Franklin, the American statesman.

The only popular life of the great Franklin written from a human standpoint for the boys and girls of America.

The True Story of Lafayette, the friend of America.

This volume, the sixth in the series of "Children's Lives of Great Men," will appeal to all young Americans. It is an absorbing, simply told, and stirring story of a remarkable character in American history, and is the "whole story," from the boyhood of the great Frenchman to the close of his long, dramatic, and romantic career.

The True Story of the United States of America. From 1492 to 1900.

This is in every sense a companion volume to the series of "Children's Lives of Great Men." It tells the true story of the beginnings, rise, and development of the republic of the United States. Its object is to tell the story of the people of America. It is largely used for home and supplementary reading, and is accepted as the most popular "story" of the United States yet told for young people.

At all bookstores, or sent postpaid on receipt of price.

LOTHROP, LEE & SHEPARD CO. • • • • **BOSTON**

Elbridge S. Brooks's Books for Boys and Girls

"Nothing deserves better of young American readers than Elbridge S. Brooks's books. . . . It is no wonder that Mr. Brooks's books are being put into so many schools, and if many such books are included 'i. school courses in the near future it is to be expected that truancy will be at a discount." — *The Interior*, Chicago.

The American Soldier. New and revised edition. Cloth, 4to, illustrated, $1.50.
A stirring and graphic record of the American fighting man, — from Bunker Hill to Santiago.

The American Sailor. New and revised edition. Cloth, 4to, illustrated, $1.50.
The only comprehensive story of the American blue-jacket, from Paul Jones to Dewey.

The American Indian. Profusely illustrated, cloth, 4to, $1.50.
The first and only complete and consecutive story of the redmen of America.

The Boy Life of Napoleon, afterwards Emperor of the French. Adapted for American children from the French of Madame Eugénie Foa. Square 8vo, illustrated, $1.25.
An absorbing and attractive volume, and the only story life of *the boy Napoleon* extant. It includes all the latest information touching upon the childhood of the most remarkable man and military leader of the nineteenth century.

In Blue and White: A Story of the American Revolution. 8vo, illustrated, $1.50.
This stirring story of the Revolution details the adventures of one of Washington's famous life-guards, who is a college mate of Alexander Hamilton, and fights in the Guard from Trenton to Yorktown.

In No Man's Land: A Wonder Story. Cloth, 12mo, illustrated, $1.00.
"Sparkles all over with glee. . . . There is not a dull line in it." — *The Dial*.

In Leisler's Times: A Story of Knickerbocker New York, told for boys and girls. Cloth, 12mo, illustrated by W. T. Smedley, $1.50.
"A good boy's book; manly, patriotic, and readable." — *The Independent*.

The Story of New York. Cloth, 8vo, illustrated, $1.50.
This initial volume of the "Story of the States Series," of which Mr. Brooks is editor.
"More like a charming fireside legend, told by a grandfather to eager children, than the dry and pompous chronicles commonly labelled history." — *Critic*, New York.

The Story of our War with Spain. Told for young Americans. One vol., 8vo, profusely illustrated, $1.50.
An authentic, complete, and reliable account of the war for Cuban liberation in 1898.
"Written in Mr. Brooks's most graphic style in simple, straightforward, stirring chronicle, without deviation for discussion or undue detail." — *The Interior*.

Storied Holidays. Cloth, 12mo, illustrated by Howard Pyle, $1.50.
A unique collection of historical stories about the world's holidays.
"A book for buying and keeping that the children as they grow up, and the parents, too, may dip into and read." — *Sunday School Times*.

At all bookstores, or sent postpaid on receipt of price.

LOTHROP, LEE & SHEPARD CO. • • • • **BOSTON**

www.ingramcontent.com/pod-product-compliance
Lightning Source LLC
Chambersburg PA
CBHW022112230426
43672CB00008B/1355